Beyond
the Blind

Beyond
the Blind

❋ Season One ❋

A Look at Life from the Duck Blind

JONATHAN PORTER

WESTBOW
PRESS
A DIVISION OF THOMAS NELSON

WestBow Press books may be ordered through booksellers or by contacting:

WestBow Press
A Division of Thomas Nelson
1663 Liberty Drive
Bloomington, IN 47403
www.westbowpress.com
1 (866) 928-1240

Because of the dynamic nature of the Internet, any web addresses or links contained in this book may have changed since publication and may no longer be valid. The views expressed in this work are solely those of the author and do not necessarily reflect the views of the publisher, and the publisher hereby disclaims any responsibility for them.

Any people depicted in stock imagery provided by Thinkstock are models, and such images are being used for illustrative purposes only. Certain stock imagery © Thinkstock.

Scripture quotations marked (NIV) are taken from the Holy Bible, New International Version®, NIV®. Copyright © 1973, 1978, 1984, 2011 by Biblica, Inc.™ Used by permission of Zondervan. All rights reserved worldwide. www.zondervan.com The "NIV" and "New International Version" are trademarks registered in the United States Patent and Trademark Office by Biblica, Inc.™

Scripture quotations marked (NASB) are taken from the New American Standard Bible®, Copyright © 1960, 1962, 1963, 1968, 1971, 1972, 1973, 1975, 1977, 1995 by The Lockman Foundation. Used by permission." (www.Lockman.org)

Scripture quotations marked (HCSB) are taken from the Holman Christian Standard Bible ® Copyright © 2003, 2002, 2000, 1999 by Holman Bible Publishers. All rights reserved.

ISBN: 978-1-4908-1699-9 (sc)
ISBN: 978-1-4908-1700-2 (hc)
ISBN: 978-1-4908-1701-9 (e)

Library of Congress Control Number: 2013921099

Printed in the United States of America.

WestBow Press rev. date: 11/21/2013

I want to dedicate this book to my family. To my wife, Gayle, for all the support through the years; there is no way that I am able to do any of what I do without you. I love you!

To my kids, Scott and Abby; I pray that you have been as blessed by me as I have been by you.

To my parents, Don and Jonnie; words can never express what you have provided me, beginning with the life that you provided me and reaching far *Beyond the Blind*.

CONTENTS

ACKNOWLEDGEMENTS

Special thanks go out to so many.
To the members of Greenville Baptist Church; thanks
for putting up with me for the last twenty years.
To Sally Neal, Sonya Gasses, and Jonnie Porter;
thanks for the hours of editing.
To Chuck Tigner; you know why I am forever grateful!
To James Underwood; for believing in a
crazy preacher and a crazy project.
To my dad for teaching me about what takes place in the
blind and for modeling what life is like beyond it!

INTRODUCTION

It was just another ordinary day. I had done everything that was on my agenda for the day and had gone to the pond close to the house to work my dog for a little while. When I got back to the house, I decided to do a little organizing. Duck season was still a couple of months away, but I thought I might get a jump on things. I went to the trailer that we take duck hunting with us and started to pull stuff out and look over what I had in the various boxes. I looked around to see my son heading out of the house and coming my way and was optimistic that maybe he would stick around and help me a bit. I proceeded to hang the waders, organize and inventory what was in the ammo box, and get rid of accumulated trash. Scott, my son, started on the coats and calls and then swept out the trailer, ridding the inside of all remnants of the south Louisiana gumbo mud that had made the 560-mile ride back with us. As we organized, straightened, and cleaned, we talked about past trips and, with a great deal of excitement, talked about what might happen in the upcoming season. As we talked, Scott looked at me and said, "Dad, you are obsessed about this stuff." I responded by telling him, "I'm not obsessed—I'm passionate." To me there is a difference.

I am passionate about many things in my life, and duck hunting is one of them. More than duck hunting, I am passionate about God, my family, and my church. Another very important passion that I have is seeing men get serious about their relationship with Jesus Christ. We live in a society where men seem to think that either there is no real need for this relationship or that it somehow makes them seem weak. The problem with this line of thinking is that when a man gets serious about what God is doing in his life, it has a direct impact on his family, his job, his community, and his church. All of these are directly affected by what a man does with his relationship with the God who created everything we enjoy as hunters and as humans.

In the Bible there is a story in the book of Acts that illustrates what I am talking about and shows clearly why I am passionate about seeing men get serious about what God is doing in their lives. In chapter 16 of Acts, there is a story about two guys named Paul and Silas. You really need to get a Bible and read this story. These two guys have an incredible encounter in a jail cell with a prison guard. After several dramatic events take place, the prison guard asks Paul and Silas what he must do to be saved, what he must do to know God personally. Paul and Silas explain everything to him, and the man begins a relationship with God. That is great in and of itself, but that is not the really cool part for me. The cool part is in verse 34 where it says, "He was filled with joy because he had come to believe in God—he and his whole family." Did you catch that? He and his whole family. You see, there is a fabulous truth here: when a man gets serious about what God is doing in his life, it directly impacts the life of his family. I have seen this many times over. When a man is leading his family, his children will follow. When a mom is bringing her kids to church all by herself, it is usually only a matter of time until we lose the kids as they get involved in something else. On the opposite side of this is the truth that when a father is bringing the family to church and staying there with them, we see time and time again that the children not only get involved but also stay involved—in many cases, for the duration of their lives. They do this because of the influence of their father.

Over the course of the pages that follow, I hope to allow my passion for duck hunting to be intertwined with my passion to see men get serious about what God can do, or may be doing, in their lives right now. I hope you enjoy the simplicity of what I have to offer you, but more importantly I hope you come to understand the abundance of what *God* has to offer you!

CHAPTER 1

Sunrise

There is something incredible about a sunrise viewed from a duck blind (or anywhere else, for that matter). You are sitting and watching for that duck to appear somewhere on the skyline. You are listening for the sound of whistling wings buzzing your head and cutting across the spread of decoys in front of you. As all of that is going on, you notice that it is happening—the sun is breaking the horizon on the eastern sky. You stop and stare.

I know that I do. So many of the pictures that I have taken over the years are of the beautiful moment when the sun appears. A new day has dawned, and with that new day come new experiences and opportunities. Even though you may have a certain expectation for that day, you still welcome the opportunity that comes with a new sunrise and a new day before you.

As I watch that sun come up over and over again, I can't help but think that the day before me is filled with new opportunities. There are moments before me to do something that I have never done before. There are other moments that I have to make something right that I omitted and that I failed to do right the first time. I don't know what that day may have before me, but I know someone who does.

Each day is a part of an unbelievable journey that I have been on since about the age of twenty-one. Every day that I live is different. My job is different from most people's in that I do something different just about every day. There are new challenges, new opportunities, new encounters, and new people that come across my path all the time. Every moment that I have is part of the plan of God.

God gave to a guy named Jeremiah an encouraging word that is found in the Bible. God said to Jeremiah, "'For I know the plans I have for you,' declares the Lord, 'plans to prosper you and not to harm you, plans to give you hope and a future'" (Jeremiah 29:11 NIV). I absolutely love that verse for several reasons. First, it reminds me that the God who causes the sun to appear every day is the same God who is enacting His plan in my life. Everything that is taking place has a purpose and brings meaning to my life. Before you go arguing that point in your mind, let me say that I don't always understand what is taking place, but that doesn't negate the fact that it is still true.

Secondly, it tells me that God wants great things for my life. I don't adhere to what I call the *prosperity gospel* or the *name it and claim it movement*, but I do believe that God wants good things to be a part of my life and to come out of my life. Thirdly, I love that God is working to bring me hope. He is navigating me through this life to position me for the future that He has had planned for me since before I was ever known about.

The great thing about this verse is that it applies to you as well. The very reasons I love this verse so much are the same reasons you should love it as well. Allow these words to permeate your mind in such a way that they transform the way you approach your future. God is working out a plan for you; He is just wanting and waiting for you to get onboard.

Remember when that sun breaks open in the eastern sky tomorrow that this day is a chance for new beginnings with incredible opportunities as you follow God. After all, He is the one who gives us the chance to start over, and my, oh my, I'm glad He does.

CHAPTER 2

A Day Like No Other

The forecast on the way to Louisiana brought a wide range of discussions and emotions. The temperature over the next few days was going to be in the teens the first day, around thirty the following day, and then drop back to the mid-teens the following two days. That can be a good thing, and it can be a bad thing in Louisiana. On the plus side, just about anytime Missouri and Arkansas get hit with a cold front coming out of the north, we usually get a good push of ducks over the next few days. That part sounded really good. The bad side of this report meant that the flooded fields that are not very deep would possibly be frozen over, giving the ducks no place to land. This in turn meant that we would have to find a way to bust the ice and make a hole or be in trouble. Additionally, the second day was calling for a complete mixture of precipitation, which can be a great thing after the four-mile four-wheeler ride to the blind.

The first day proved to be quite a challenge. The skies were blue, but the water was frozen. I broke as much ice as I could break to create a hole, but it seemed to freeze back right away. We scratched out a few, but nowhere close to our limits.

As the day progressed, we did a little scouting and found the temps rising and the water thawing. In the midst of this change, the clouds were forming as the ducks were arriving. With great anticipation, we went to bed praying for a good morning.

As the second day broke, the forecast was right on. We had rain, sleet, and snow all during the course of the morning, with a nice north wind cutting to our core. As miserable as the weather was making things, the hunting began with a bang. This was one of the mornings I will never forget. The green-winged teal were flying at daybreak, and mixtures of mallards, gadwalls, and spoonbills were not far behind. It was hard to see anything with sleet and snow coming down, but we kept our eyes peeled anyway.

What amazing sights we saw all morning as flocks of birds cut through the storms to buzz our decoys. Flocks of twenty, thirty, and forty birds zigzagged through the storm, battling the elements to see what was calling to them. Those images still get me going today. It was nothing short of spectacular.

A group of guys known as the disciples followed Jesus and did ministry with Him just about every day for three years. One night when these men were out in a boat, a great storm came up rather quickly. As the storm raged, these guys feared for their lives. In the midst of the storm, they saw something that appeared to be a ghost or something that they didn't want to see up close. They were, to say the least, terrified. It was in the middle of this storm that they heard these words: "Take courage! It is I. Don't be afraid" (Matthew 14:27 NIV). These words spoken by Jesus were all they needed to find the strength to continue on, the peace to compose themselves, and the hope to weather the storm they found themselves in.

These are the same words that we need to hear to help us weather the storms we face every day. These storms are brought on by financial stress, marital problems, professional challenges, family issues, and a host of other things in life. Will you hear Jesus say to you, "Take courage"? We need to be courageous in our marriages and in our families. We need courage to do the right things in our workplaces and social settings. As men, we need to be courageous in our faith, now more than ever before. He reminds us that He is with us in the midst of the storm, even when we don't know that He is there. Knowing that He is there alleviates our fears and brings hope and peace to our lives. I promise you that He is there.

Maybe you need to look through the storms that are raging around you. You will see the evidence of His presence. Maybe you need to open your ears and hear as He speaks to you in the midst of life's storms. Those men heard Jesus speak those words on that night. I believe that when you start to listen, you will hear Jesus speak to you in whatever storm you find yourself in right now. Are you looking? Are you listening? He is there! I promise!

CHAPTER 3

A Bad Start to a Good Day

Many people reading this understand what it is like in a duck blind leading up to shooting light. There are those moments when you are getting everything lined up. I know for me, I want my shells to be in the right place for easy access. I want my gun to be at my right hand. When I put my call lanyard around my neck, I want it to be a certain way where the calls are arranged for easy access to my left hand. I want everything else stored neatly out of the way but so I can still have access to my blind bag (and maybe the bag we call the *snack wagon*). Of course, I want all that done well before shooting light, so I can stand and watch the skyline as daybreak appears. I can then soak in that magical moment when everything starts to come alive with the first sounds of wings cutting through the air, long before I spot the first flock of birds moving past or circling around. You get the picture.

I am on a hunt that has become an annual hunt where my buddy and I get to take our dads and join with some great friends that I have come to know over the last ten years. On this day as all of those predawn preparations were taking place, I was with two good friends in Marksville, Louisiana, hunting when everything kind of broke loose.

Beyond the Blind

All of a sudden my lifelong friend Kyle jumps up and leans across me as far as he can get. I started to punch him but gave him the benefit of the doubt and asked him what the heck he was doing before I punched. He looks back over his shoulder to where he was sitting and asks me what that was on the shelf that had been just over his right shoulder. As I shot a beam of light over there, I saw the scaly skin of a snake going back behind a shell box. Being the fond lover of snakes that I am, I exited the blind in a short amount of time with Kyle not far behind me. The third person with me that day was a little braver than the two of us, but not all that thrilled about our circumstances. He took the handle of a broom and began a mission of removing the intruder from our midst.

As all of this is taking place and Kyle and I are standing waist deep in water in our waders, we begin to see the first flight of ducks and know that we are missing a great opportunity to start the day off right. Our kind host, Mike, succeeds in the snake removal and we get back into position to start the hunt with a few laughs along the way. As we talked I scanned the water to see the beast that was just thrown out from among us swimming right back to the blind. Shortly thereafter, meaning a couple seconds, the first shot of the morning was fired. One snake down, eighteen ducks to go. I was bound and determined that this ugly beast wasn't going to mess up a good day for me.

Snakes have the potential to ruin a great day. It almost happened to us. The fact is, though, that it happens to many of us all the time. In the first book of the Bible, there is a reference to a snake that ruins not only people's day, but ruins people's lives. It says in Genesis that "the serpent was more crafty than any of the wild animals the Lord God had made" (Genesis 3:1 NIV). The snake here is Satan, and he is so crafty and deceitful that it is hard to comprehend. The last book in the Bible is Revelation, and there are words found there as well that describe what Satan does. Revelation says that "The great dragon was hurled down—that ancient serpent called the devil, or Satan, who leads the whole world astray" (Revelation 12:9 NIV). The sole purpose of Satan is to lead people away from God and ruin their lives. It is Satan that tries to destroy marriages, divide families, and tempts men with pornography and sexual temptations. It is Satan that urges each of us to move away from the things that God has in store for us and ultimately to bring negative things to our lives.

How did Kyle see that snake since it was behind him? Glad you asked. Out of the corner of his eye he saw movement and the fluttering of the snake's tongue, which of course prompted him to lean as far away from it and across me. Now we look closer every time we get in the blind. The same is true for our lives. We must look to make sure that Satan has no room to work. We have to recognize what he is trying to do and get rid of him as quickly as we can. The only way we can do this is through disciplines like prayer, Bible study, and worship. These play a vital role in making sure that Satan doesn't have any place to work in our lives.

I know some of the farmers around me tell me about the good snakes and the bad snakes and, yes, I know that they are right. I also know that there is an old phrase that says the only good snake is a dead snake. When I am hunting I am always on the lookout for snakes for the sake of myself, those hunting with me, and my dogs. I am also on the lookout in my everyday life for the snake that is always around. I watch out for that snake more for myself, my wife, my kids, and my church. As long as I know he is around, he can't hurt me. When I think he is not around, that's when I will get bit. Spot him and get rid of him, and you will find yourself with more good days than bad!

CHAPTER 4

Look Out Below!

The hunt had been a good one. We were back in a familiar place in North Louisiana with the crew that I had been hunting with for a few years. We all had a great time on our first morning out. Most of the places I go are accessible by a four-wheeler as I hunt in many places where there are flooded fields, levees, and pit blinds. Well, the hunt was over, the pictures were taken, and the four-wheelers were being loaded up as we prepared for our ride back to camp. As the last things were loaded, we were ready to pull out. It was then that *it* happened. *It* was one of the funniest things that I have ever seen after I found out that everything was okay.

My buddy Chuck loaded up on his four-wheeler and proceeded to move it out of the way for everyone else to load up. Unbeknownst to him, the four-wheeler was in reverse. As he mashed on the gas, the Honda shot backward, running into the duck blind with a wheel hovering over the dog box on the end of the blind. You will have to picture this in your mind because I didn't have a camera handy to catch this moment. Chuck is now leaning as far forward as he can while looking back with a look of sheer terror. The rest of us ran over and pushed the bike off the blind and got all the wheels back on level ground. It was at this point that I almost split my side laughing. As this moment replayed over and over in my head, I just kept laughing. Everyone was doing the same except, of course, Chuck who found no humor in this situation and rightfully wanted to know who left the four-wheeler in reverse to begin with.

There are many moments in life that cause us fear. Those moments may be self-induced, or they may be brought on by circumstances out of our control. The reason behind our fear is almost irrelevant to the feelings fear brings. As men, we don't like to admit that fear even exists in our lives. There is, however, a fear that each of us ought to have present in our lives.

The writer of the Old Testament book of Proverbs gives us these words: "The fear of the Lord is the beginning of wisdom" (Proverbs 9:10 NIV). To *fear* the Lord is to stand in awe of who He is. It means that we are to recognize the character that is completely God and then respond with lives that have a reverence for Him exemplified by how much we trust Him, serve Him, and worship Him. This is a starting point for many great things to happen within our lives as we fear the Lord. This fear is a healthy fear. This fear helps keep things in perspective for each of us as we navigate the terrain of this thing we call life.

The question is, How is the fear factor in your life? Do you have a deep reverence for God, and are you responding appropriately with your life? Never forget that this is a starting point, and it produces wisdom that only God can place in your life. What do you know? Fear can be a good thing!

CHAPTER 5

Don't Be Afraid to Ask

I have been duck hunting a long time, but I still have so much to learn. When I hunt with guys who I know are experienced, I often start out a little slow. I guess you could say that I get a little intimidated. I really don't want to mess up, so I ease into the hunt. I'm not that way at all around my friends, but new guys and men that are more knowledgeable, well, you know how it is. One of the joys of the hunting brotherhood is that I have found very few people who are unwilling to answer questions or teach you some new tricks along the way. I have had the privilege of hunting with some outstanding men in my lifetime, and I have learned and continue to learn from many of them still today.

There is one guy who has taught me a lot about calling. Another friend taught me about decoy spreads. Yet another has helped me learn about habitat. A friend down the road helps me each year with shooting tips as we practice out on his skeet range. There are others, several in fact, who give me tips on training my dog and keeping him tuned up for the upcoming season. There are so many more that I really can't go into full detail due to the fact that each person seems to give me a little more. Of course, I can't help but mention all that my dad taught me and his dad, my grandfather, with the most important being a genuine love for the outdoors and all that God gave us in it.

We also live in an age of technology. This high tech world has gotten so simple that even I can use and take advantage of it now. My family laughs at the shows that I watch on the Outdoor Channel as well as others. I have a full library of videos that I watch, mostly before each season. Then there is the Internet and YouTube where I can search for so many things. I sit and watch, and every time I do, I learn a little bit more about this thing that I love. You see, learning can be a great thing. It always helps to have more knowledge.

There was a guy named Paul who taught a guy named Timothy about all kinds of things concerning God and the church. Paul instructed young Timothy one day to "Do your best to present yourself to God as one approved, a worker who does not need to be ashamed and who correctly handles the word of truth" (2 Timothy 2:15 NIV). He wanted Timothy to study so that he might know all that he needed to. Then, whatever came his way, he would be prepared. God wants us prepared. That is why He gave us the Bible. This incredible book gives us everything God wanted us to know about Himself. The question logically follows: How much do you know?

If we as men are going to have a healthy marriage, we better understand what God's intention for marriage is really all about. If we want to be good fathers to our children, then we need to get some parenting advice from the One who gave us our children. If we want to succeed in the world where the marketplace is competitive, we better get the wisdom in our head that God offers us. If we are to have a life that is full of meaning, then we better understand the meaning of life from the one who gives us life. I think you are starting to get the picture.

If we are going to put the time in to make sure that our hunt is a success, don't you think we ought to put the time in to make sure our life is a success as well? Paul had the answer for young Timothy, and he has the answer for us. Dive in and discover what God has waiting for you. I promise it is worth the effort!

CHAPTER 6

Snack Wagon Coming Through

I would like to take this moment to thank our two primary sponsors. The first shout-out goes to Dr. Pepper. You know I am not a coffee drinker, and all those early mornings after getting set up and waiting for shooting time, you have been there to pick me up and get me going. Words cannot express my gratitude for all you have done through the years. Secondly, I would like to thank Little Debbie. Although we have never met, I feel as though we have known one another for years. You too have been there every time I needed you. You have given and given of yourself without me having to even ask. Your Honey Buns, Pecan Spinwheels, Nutty Bars, Swiss Rolls, just to name a few, have seen me through many hungry moments until I could safely return to the camp and consume some sort of other unhealthy food associated with each trip I make. Oh wait, I almost omitted one other sponsor. I am truly sorry! I must give Hostess a shout-out. Where would I be without your Donettes, both chocolate and powdered? How many times did you see me through with a neatly wrapped Ding Dong or Twinkie? I am so grateful.

Beyond the Blind

If the video I never made or the TV show I never produced ever won an award, I guess that would be the totality of my speech of gratitude. In actuality, I wish those companies would sponsor my trips. It would save me a lot of money.

There are several bags that have made the trips with us every year. Those different bags have assumed the same nickname: *snack wagon*. The snack wagon is that which goes on the four-wheeler before the shell bag gets loaded. It is loaded down with deer jerky, sunflower seeds, drinks of all kinds, loads of unhealthy junk food, and a few other things that may or may not have an expired freshness date on it. When someone in the blind is hungry, you simply ask for the snack wagon to come your way. It may come in a hurry or it may take a few minutes to get there as the other hands dip into the wagon on its journey. One thing is for sure, the snack wagon gets us through some long mornings and on more than one occasion has gotten us through days when we stayed from early morning to sunset. On those days, we were always grateful for the snack wagon and its contents.

The downside of this approach is that after duck season, I don't even want to see another sugary snack cake or morsel of junk food. I have gotten tired of eating that kind of stuff and want something with real substance.

Jesus actually had something to say along these lines. Jesus had been in the wilderness for forty days and nights, and during that time He had not eaten. He had become very hungry in that Jesus was fully man even though He was still fully God. The hunger was intense, and Satan decided to tempt Him to turn stones into bread so He could eat. Jesus said in chapter 4 of Matthew: "It is written: 'Man shall not live on bread alone, but on every word that comes from the mouth of God'" (Matthew 4:4 NIV).

Jesus was actually quoting a verse found in the first part of the Bible, the Old Testament, in Deuteronomy 8:3. Both of these references are there to remind us how important God's Word really is. When I refer to God's Word, I am referring to the Bible. This is where lives can really take a turn in the right direction. We need substance, not junk. God's Word is the substance we need.

It's important for every man to know and understand the Bible. God gave us His words so that we might understand life and its meaning in a much greater way. Too often, people approach this book with the thought process that says, "If you read this and follow what it says, then your life will be limited." I would contend to you that it is the exact opposite. When you understand what God is communicating to you through the words that He gave you, then you really start to live with true freedom. There is inherent in every instruction that God gives, a blessing for our lives for following that instruction. By reading and understanding the Bible, you are actually gaining insight into the plan, the purpose, and the meaning that God has for your life. It really is time for men to step up to the plate and get serious about this. Get a good Bible (I even have one in camo) in a translation that is easy to read. Start reading in the New Testament. John happens to be one of my favorite books to read in the Bible. Ask questions from guys you know who are involved in Bible study of their own. Get involved in a men's Bible study at a church near you or at your church. This is a great starting point. Take this challenge. Start reading your Bible and ask God to give you insights that will enable you to understand what is going on in your life in a much clearer manner. Do this for thirty days. You can do anything for thirty days. I promise you that after thirty days, you will not want to stop because this is one challenge that will radically affect your life. Are you up to the challenge? Then *go*! What are you waiting for?

We really can't live on snack foods, junk food, or bread alone. We must live our lives in accordance with every word that comes from the mouth of God. Then and only then can you really live!

CHAPTER 7

Listen Up!

When I was a teenager, my dad and I belonged to a hunting club that had properties all over the place. One of the reasons that my dad decided to get us into this particular club was our love of waterfowl hunting, and this club had numerous properties throughout the south Louisiana area and in particular in the southwest area of our state. In this area the waterfowling has an excellent reputation for many different species of waterfowl. In this area it is not uncommon to get a chance at teal, gadwall, pintail, mallard, widgeon, and shovelers, as well as snow geese, blue geese, and specklebelly geese. This area is notorious for great hunting.

My dad got the idea since this particular farm we were going to had pit blinds that were fairly comfortable, it would be a great chance to take my mom with us and show her what all the fuss was about. After all, we got to take the three-wheeler out to the blind. (You know how old this story is now since four-wheelers weren't around yet.) We had a nice place to sit and Mom wouldn't get muddy or anything, and I guess for those reasons she decided to go with us. The morning came and off we went to our chosen blind. We set out decoys, got Mom settled in the blind, got the dog set up on the end and waited for daybreak. The birds were moving and Dad and I were pretty pumped about the morning. Shooting time came and the hunt began. Everything was going great for the first twenty to thirty minutes as the birds buzzed the decoys and the dog did what he was trained to do. Mom, of course, did not share the same enthusiasm for what was taking place as we did, so she was lying down on the bench to get comfortable until the hunt was over. As I stood watching for more birds I heard Mom speak words that I will have etched in my mind for a long, long time. All she said was: "Jonathan, don't move." I knew right then that something wasn't right and I had better listen to what she said. As I looked down to see what she was talking about, I saw now what was not visible thirty minutes earlier: a three-foot cottonmouth water moccasin coiled up a few feet away from my foot. Many things ran through my head as I slowly moved in the opposite direction. Dad told me to unload and use the butt of my gun to kill the snake, but I was a little too shaken up for that. All in all, Dad took care of the problem and we got back to hunting. One thing is for sure, I am glad that I obeyed when Mom spoke that day!

There is always a blessing for our obedience. Jesus was speaking one day and He said these words: "Blessed rather are those who hear the word of God and obey it" (Luke 11:28 NIV). Notice that He used the word *blessed*. There is always a blessing for obedience. Growing up, too many people view the Bible as nothing more that a set of rules and regulations that limit what they can do and how much fun they can have doing it. I want you to see that behind every instruction or principle you find in God's word is a promise of blessing for obeying it. Jesus knew that many people would hear His words, but He really wanted people to act upon those words because He knew that their lives would be enhanced and changed the more they obeyed them.

That is exactly what He wants for you today. He wants you to hear that He speaks to you and He wants you to obey them. The more we obey, the better our lives turn out to be. There is so much that all of us have to learn, myself first and foremost. Hearing what God has to say is a great place to start that process of learning. I hope that you will see that many times His words are there to protect you just as my mom's words were for me that day. Other times, His words are there to direct you, to encourage you, to instruct you, to help you, to answer your questions, or simply to let you know that He cares about what is going on in your life because He cares about you. Listen up—He may just be changing your life right now!

CHAPTER 8

It Couldn't Be, Could It?

O ne of the joys of watching my son grow up was watching the progression that took place over his life. Many of you reading this know exactly what I mean. There was a time when we went hunting and he took a BB gun just to feel like he was one of the guys. Then came the time when I taught him how to handle a single-shot 20-gauge and let him go out of the blind and finish off the cripples. He progressed from there to a youth-model 20-gauge semiauto where he got to stand on a box and shoot (which is the same phase I went through where I didn't get to shoot very much as I watched over him for safety reasons). This is where the story got a little funny one day.

We were in North Louisiana for a hunt right after Thanksgiving when Scott, my son, was about ten years old. As we got set up, longtime friend and duck guide Johnny Wink asked Scott to come down and sit by him. He told him he could help him watch for the ducks, learn to blow a duck call, and they would shoot all the ducks before they could get to us. Naturally, Scott took him up on the offer. Johnny gave me a little grin and I gave him a nod of thanks for not only showing my son a good time, but also for letting me get some shooting in.

Just after first light, we were scanning the horizon for ducks and had already pulled the trigger on a few and had a few in the blind. It was around this time that Johnny stood and looked to the west and, much to his surprise, saw a snow goose sitting on the water about 150 yards from the blind. The goose just sat there motionless, prompting me and others to surmise that it was a decoy that had gotten loose during a storm. Johnny assured us that it was no decoy and told Scott to put the sneak attack on it. Scott looked at him as if he had lost his already crazy mind. Johnny continued to prod him to go, and Scott continued to look at me for a nod of approval. After assessing the situation, I gave him the go-ahead. After all, he knew how to handle his gun, and this was a chance he had never had before in his childhood. Scott got out of the blind, retrieved his youth-model 20-gauge from Johnny, and off he went. He eased down the levee ever so slowly with everyone in the blind watching him. As he closed the distance to about fifty yards, the goose sat up and began to swim away. Scott picked up the pace a bit and after closing to about thirty yards, he pulled up his gun and fired a perfect shot. He was thrilled to say the least. He set his gun down and waded out in his waders to get his prize snow goose. He could truly say that he had done this all by himself. As he came back to the blind, I will never forget his facial expression as he beamed with joy, and I will never forget what he told Johnny. He got settled back in, answered everyone's questions, and gave out a few high fives. He then looked at Johnny and said "I almost didn't go because I didn't believe the goose was real. I sure am glad I went anyway!" That was priceless for me as a dad, and I know Johnny enjoyed it as well.

There are times in life when it is hard to believe that our circumstances are real both on the positive side and the negative. For many men, myself included, it is hard to listen to what someone else has to say. It is not because we think we know it all. Many times it is because we want to accomplish something on our own. Other times, we want to do things the way that we know how and not complicate the matter. Then there are times when we simply don't ask or seek other opinions because we are ashamed of our circumstances and don't want to admit that for some reason we have failed or faltered. There is a verse in the Old Testament of the Bible in Proverbs, chapter 3, that tells us, "Trust in the Lord with all your heart and lean not on your own understanding" (Proverbs 3:5 NIV). There are so many times that I just had to trust God when I didn't know the answers. There were times when I didn't have money to pay for a bill and somehow God provided what I needed, as well as many other stories just the same.

One time a guy gave me $150 right after I spoke at a small meeting. He didn't even know why he was giving it to me other than the fact that God led him to do so. As I made my way home I got a call from my wife that our car had broken down. I told her who to call and not to worry about it. The problem was the alternator, and a church member fixed it for me. As you might have already guessed, the cost to fix the car was $152 and change. My cost was just under three dollars. God knew what I needed before I knew what I needed. That is just the way He works. It seems easier to trust ourselves, but that really gets me nowhere. I have to trust God. Just as Scott had to trust that day in the duck blind and take that step of faith, so also we must trust God in our everyday lives and take steps of faith that allow Him to work in our lives.

Scott experienced a great moment that beautiful morning as he got his first ever snow goose. He will remember that for the rest of his life. You too can experience great moments that you will remember the rest of your life when you stop relying on your own understanding of things in your life and start trusting God with your mind and with your heart. Are you ready? On your mark, get set, *go!* The rest of your life is waiting, and so is God.

CHAPTER 9

There Ain't No Way!

To those who are reading this with a propensity toward correct grammar, you are already lost at the title alone. Well, there really wasn't another title that accurately described what this little story is all about.

A few years ago, after some careful planning, I was able to go in with a few guys and secure several duck blinds in the southwest area of Louisiana. There were going to be many advantages to this, such as being able to go when I wanted, being able to take my son and schedule around his basketball schedule, being able to develop new friendships, as well as a host of other things. One of the big advantages of this particular set up was the ability to add two weeks to my duck season, and that was the early September teal season. I had not been able to take advantage of this part of duck hunting since I moved out of Louisiana in 1986. Duck hunting had taken a backseat to deer and turkey hunting when I moved to Georgia due to the fact that duck hunting just wasn't the same here. After a few years, I missed duck hunting, and as my kids grew, I was able to get back into it, and how glad I am that I did. (My wife may have a different opinion.) Having said all that, adding in teal season was a huge bonus and never has conflicted with my son's basketball schedule.

The first year I was able to teal hunt on my new lease, my son and I were hunting with a local guy I had just met. As it was my first trip to this farm to hunt, I had not yet learned the layout or tactics or much of anything for that matter other than my initial scouting visit. This guy's name was Troy, and he knew just what to do and just what to bring. After we met everyone at the camp, we ventured out to the blind for the morning hunt. If you have never been in Louisiana, then you really can't comprehend the magnitude of the mosquitoes that are there. They are numerous. They are large. They are aggressive, and they are annoying. As we settled into the blind and mosquitoes began to rise up out of the blind like geese coming off a grain field, Troy pulled out this gadget called a ThermaCELL. Now you must understand that I grew up in Louisiana and I had hunted ducks as a kid and used everything known to mankind to combat these vicious creatures, and nothing in my experience had worked. Troy lights this thing as I ask what it is. He explains it to me as I am steadily slapping these vipers off my skin and considering mounting a couple of the big ones. As Troy sets this gadget in the middle of the blind, I am thinking to myself, "There ain't no way!" There is no way that this thing is going to drive away all these mosquitoes in such a way that they won't bother us all morning. Well, as they say, it takes a big man to admit when he is wrong. I am a big man. I was wrong. Within a few minutes, there appeared to be an invisible barrier around me with these nasty pests now several feet over my head but not around me. It was a miracle, and I was now in the market for a new gadget that would not leave my blind bag.

My problem was doubt. I was very doubtful that this new gadget would work. There are several things in life that I do not doubt. A ThermaCELL is now on my list. It's not at the top of the list, but it is on the list. At the top of the *No Doubt* list is God and the relationship I have with Him. As much as there are times that I don't understand what God is doing or how He is doing it, I don't doubt God. He has never let me down. He has been there for me time and time again when I didn't know where to turn or what to do next. There is a guy named James in the Bible who talks about doubt. James happens to be the half brother of Jesus. He writes in the first chapter these words:

"But when you ask, you must believe and not doubt, because the one who doubts is like a wave of the sea, blown and tossed by the wind. That person should not expect to receive anything from the Lord. Such a person is double-minded and unstable in all they do." (James 1:6–8 NIV)

We live in a society where many don't even make it to doubting whether or not God will do something—they doubt whether He even exists. We move from there to those who believe He does exist but doubt that He will step in and do anything. James says that this type of person is unstable in all they do because they really don't know what they are all about. Our faith as men needs to be grounded in the presence of God. When we seek God, we need to ask with that belief that He will answer and trust Him when He answers in a way that differs from what we think should happen. You see the crazy thing here is that God is going to be God whether we want to believe that or not. He is going to be God whether we want to trust Him or not. I think I'm going with believing in who He says He is and believing that He is capable of doing all things in my life. He can! He wants to! He will! The catch to it is found in what James says to each of us: "You must believe and not doubt" (v. 6).

I believe a ThermaCELL gadget can take care of those pesky south Louisiana mosquitoes, and I believe that God can take care of all those pesky problems I face in life. How about you?

CHAPTER 10

What a Great Surprise

I made an impromptu trip to Baton Rouge over the Christmas break so see a longtime friend and his family. My kids really wanted to go and see some of their friends, so I told them I would take them and off we went. I did, at the last minute, grab my shell bag, waders, and shotgun on the off chance that I might get in a duck hunt while I was down that way.

On one of my annual hunts with some good friends, I am told year after year to come back, but quite honestly I never like to impose, so I don't call to ask if I can come. My buddy Kyle was who I was staying with, and he probably couldn't go anyway. As it turned out, he could go, so I made the call to see if any blinds were open for the next morning that we could slide into for a quick hunt. The answer was *yes* so we started to make some quick plans. We left Baton Rouge late that night and made the drive to our friend's camp, getting in around midnight. We hopped up early with a plan to hunt, hopefully get our limits quickly, and head back to Baton Rouge. That was the plan, but you know how plans go!

We were hunting with another friend named Bill that morning, and we got off to a good start. Like many mornings however, the hunting got a little slow after first flight. This is usually the time the snack bag comes out, and we pass the time with a quick snack waiting on the next movement of birds. The problem was there was no snack bag. This was to be a quick hunt, and neither Kyle not I brought anything to munch on during the slow moments. About the time that I was making this startling revelation and my stomach was confirming my observations with some rumblings, Bill pulls out a tin foil package, lights a heater behind us, and throws the package on the top. The tin foil begins to heat up and a very nice aroma fills the blind. Bill reaches back and opens up the foil and then reveals the fact that he has brought a Cajun specialty to the blind called boudin. Boudin is made of pork, rice, a variety of spices, all stuffed back into the pork casing, and might I say it is delicious. That morning it was extra good. I don't know that life could have gotten any better at that point: hunting with friends, eating boudin, and enjoying God's creation.

Beyond the Blind

It is precisely settings like that where I am reminded of what James wrote in the New Testament where he writes, "Every good and perfect gift is from above, coming down from the Father of the heavenly lights, who does not change like shifting shadows" (James 1:17 NIV). As James wrote under God's inspiration, he reminds each of us that every good thing that we have in life is a direct result of the activity of God. God is so incredible that He wants to do and give good things to those who are seeking Him and following Him. He has a way of working in our lives that can just blow us away. One of the gifts that I love is watching a beautiful sunrise from the duck blind. I have so many pictures of this scene and every one to me is a gift. It reminds me that God is always on my side. It shows me that God is always looking out for my best interest. This verse reminds me that God is a God of perfection and greatness. There is never a moment when God is not aware of what is happening in my life and responding from the depths of His greatness. Look around! What are the gifts that He has given you? Maybe you never looked at it like that before, or maybe you never thought about it like that before, but when you begin to see events and circumstances of your life from this perspective, it will in no small way affect how you approach life from here on out. So stop! Look around! Realize that every good and perfect gift comes from God because He loves you and wants the best for you!

CHAPTER 11

Stay Alert

One of our neighbors was in the same hunting club that my father and I were in but for a completely different reason. This club literally had properties all over America, and our neighbor wanted to deer hunt more than anything else. We had been out to Texas on a trip with him and told him various tales (most of them true) about our time hunting waterfowl. He had done some waterfowl hunting in the past and was somewhat knowledgeable about what he was doing. He really wanted to go, so we set up a hunt over in Southwest Louisiana, where we could hunt ducks and geese.

On this particular morning, I do remember the hunting to be very slow. We had our blind, and our neighbor was in a blind with someone else. I don't remember killing very much that day, but I do vividly remember what happened later in the morning.

Dad and I gave up and decided to hit the road after a slow hunt. We gathered our gear and went to see what our friend was going to do. If he was ready, we were going to grab some lunch on the way out and make the two-and-a-half-hour drive back to the house. As we approached his blind, we slowed down and watched a nice flock of specklebelly geese work the back side of the field. As the group of birds worked back and forth, I watched and listened to see what the guys in the blind were doing. I heard no calls, and I saw no movement. The birds took just the right turn and moved right toward the blind. My dad and I sat watching with great anticipation of what was about to take place. Any second now, the guys would call the shot, jump and shoot, and with some good shooting, Dad and I would take our dog over and help them with the retrieves. Here it comes ... time to shoot! Nothing! Not a shot was fired! The geese just continued to meander back and forth to the far end of the field, where they would light and feed for a while. Dad and I made our way to the blind and of course asked them why they didn't shoot. I will always remember the response as they said, "We never saw them until it was too late."

In my line of work as a pastor, I hear that line about life quite often coming from many people but especially men. Many people encounter difficulties, and they don't know what to do because they were taken by surprise. They were taken off guard by their circumstances and now do not know what to do or where to turn. Maybe it is a marriage that is going bad. There are warning signs that have been missed, and now you don't know what to do. Maybe it is the job where you have been struggling. There are other parts of our lives, such as parenting, friends, responsibilities as a child with aging parents, and a host of others. Life has a way of allowing things to jump up and bite us. At least that's what we like to say or think.

There are a couple of verses that I want to share with you here. The first one is found in a book of the Bible called 1 Peter that tells us, "Be alert and of sober mind. Your enemy the Devil prowls around like a roaring lion looking for someone to devour" (1 Peter 5:8 NIV). Peter tells us point-blank that there is a force out there that is constantly undermining our lives. That force is an evil force, and God calls that force Satan or the Devil. Satan loves it when he rips apart a marriage.

He loves it when he orchestrates moments that draw someone away from God. He thrives on destroying people's lives and getting them to blame or question God for what is taking place. That is who he is. Peter equates him to a roaring lion that is on the prowl for something that he can consume or devour. You have seen that picture before somewhere, I know. That is who he is and that is what he does. Therefore Peter instructs us to *be alert*. He tells us that so we might watch for the warning signs of marriage problems. He wants us to see financial challenges before becoming financially ruined. He longs for us to be alert to what is happening on the lives of our children before it is too late. It is for these very situations and more that he tells us to *be alert*.

The second verse is found a few books back from this passage in 1 Corinthians: "Be on your guard; stand firm in the faith; be courageous; be strong" (1 Corinthians 16:13 NIV). A guy named Paul wrote these words as God instructed him to. He tells us to *be on guard*. The thought process is the same here. We must constantly be on guard against anything that can bring destruction and pain into our lives. Those things can creep in our homes and into our lives through books, videos, the Internet, a friend, coworker, or just about any other avenue you can think of. In order to win in every area of our lives, we must look closely at this verse and apply it quickly. In order to win, we must not only be on guard, but we must also be courageous and strong. Life is not easy. It requires that we make good and wise choices and that we are willing to stand by those things. We must be smart enough and wise enough to see the problems coming.

Then we must be courageous enough and strong enough to win the battles that come our way. It all begins, however, with being *alert*! Never stop being alert. You will be able to embrace all that is good and defeat all that is bad, but you have to see those things coming in order to do both, so ... *be alert*!

CHAPTER 12

That Stench Is Awful

The setting is *beautiful*. My dad and I are in a pit blind south of Lake Charles, Louisiana. The sky is clear, and the hint of daylight is on the horizon. It is going to be a *bluebird* morning, meaning that the sky is going to be bright blue with few clouds, a lot of sunshine, and the birds should be working nicely very soon. Everything was set and we were checking our watches to see how long we were going to have to wait. The great thing about this morning is that we were getting to hunt with our new Black Lab, Gator, who was now about ten months old. As I got out of the blind to make some last minute adjustments to the decoy spread, Gator spotted something moving on the horizon and decided it was too much for him not to go check out. This was before the days of shock collars, so as he broke and I called, there wasn't much I could do to stop him when he refused to listen. It was just a few moments before he arrived at the prey and his curiosity was satisfied in a not-so-pleasant way. What Gator encountered that beautiful morning was nothing less that a nice, big, fat, juicy skunk. Pepe the skunk did what skunks do best, and Gator was quickly en route back to the blind, this time carrying quite the smell. Let me tell you something, mister, that stench was awful. We had not even fired the first shot, and the morning was just about ruined.

I really don't remember if we killed any ducks or geese that morning. All I remember is how bad that dog smelled. He sat by me in his dog box and it was all I could do to hunt. I failed to mention that we had driven down the night before in a conversion van that we slept in, and Gator had to ride home all two and a half hours inside that van with our windows cracked during the dead of winter trying to breath. The crazy part was that, if he would have just listened to me, the whole incident could have been avoided and that stench would have never been on him.

The same is true of our approach to God. If we would listen to Him, we could avoid many things in life that bring about bad consequences. When we disobey God, sin becomes a part of our lives and the consequences of that sin stain our lives and leave a stench. In the Old Testament of the Bible, God spoke to a guy named Jeremiah and said these words:

> "Although you wash yourself with soap
> and use an abundance of cleansing powder,
> the stain of your guilt is still before me,"
> declares the Sovereign Lord. (Jeremiah 2:22 NIV)

God sees and knows our sin. He knows when we have failed to listen and heed what He was trying to get us to do. He knows when we failed to follow when He was trying to protect us from something that was going to be harmful to us and leave a stench. The fact of the matter is this: we can't hide sin from God. He knows our hearts better than we know our hearts. He knows our minds better than we know our minds. He understands our lives better than we can ever begin to understand it ourselves. He knows that sin, when left in our lives, will bring tragic consequences. To the guy who thinks no one knows about his affair, God does. To the guy who thinks no sees what he is looking at on the computer, God does. To the guy who thinks no one knows he is skimming from his company, God does. You get the point. God knows everything about us and knows the mess that sin gets us into in life.

Because God knows all these things, He has also taken steps to help us in the midst of all this. In 1 John, the Bible says, "If we confess our sins, He is faithful and just and will forgive us our sins and purify us from all unrighteousness" (1 John 1:9 NIV).

What each man has to do for himself is confess his sin before God and ask God to forgive him. It really isn't that hard. When we do this, there is a promise that follows. It clearly says that God is great enough and faithful enough to forgive our sin and to make our life clean again in his sight.

Psalm 103:12 tells us that not only does God forgive sin, but he casts it as far away as "the east is from the west." God promises to remove all sin from us and cast it so far away that He won't remember it anymore. The prerequisite to that is our confession before Him. We must first come to God in prayer, confessing what we have done and asking His forgiveness. When we do that, our lives take a sudden leap toward a better and brighter future with a bluebird sky and no stench that we have to endure. If you haven't, take some time to get right with God. It's a *game changer!*

CHAPTER 13

Pirogue Plus

There were so many mornings when I was growing up that my dad and I went to one of our favorite places near where my grandparents lived to hunt ducks. My grandparents lived in a small town south of New Orleans, Louisiana, called Paradis. A short drive away is another town called Boutte, Louisiana, and that is where I first learned the joys of duck hunting. Of course, at the age of six, there wasn't much for me to do except sit and ride and be as still as possible. Our method of transportation to and from the blind through the south Louisiana marsh was a pirogue. In case you don't know what that is, it is basically a flat bottom canoe that is used to get through the very shallow waters of the marsh. You can paddle a pirogue, but mostly a push pole is used as you stand and push yourself in the pirogue to your destination. As a young boy, I never thought much about it. I remember getting to the blind on more than one occasion and seeing my dad sweating bullets, but then again that was not that uncommon in south Louisiana even during duck season. As I grew older and had a son of my own and started to do things for him, the reality of all that my father had done began to sink in. All those mornings, the pirogue was loaded down with all kinds of gear for the hunt. We had shell boxes, bags of decoys, shotguns, not to mention a small boy, a Black Lab Retriever, and a grown man with a push pole. No wonder he was sweating even in the cold temperatures when we got to the blind. The coolest revelation for me was not so much that he did all that, but that he did all that for me. I now live in Georgia and hunt in Louisiana. I make an eight-hour drive one way to our lease several times a year. Considering how much I love to hunt, it's not just about the hunt anymore. It has become more about getting to spend that time with my son and give him the same experiences that I was able to enjoy with my father. I know he doesn't get it now, just like I didn't get it then, but he will one day and will be better for it.

There is a passage in the book of Matthew in the Bible found in chapter 7 that says "Which of you, if your son asks for bread, will give him a stone? Or if he asks for a fish, will give him a snake? If you, then, though you are evil, know how to give good gifts to your children, how much more will your Father in heaven give good gifts to those who ask him!" (Matthew 7:9–11 NIV). Those verses kind of make me go *wow!* Of all the things that my father did for me as I was growing up, my Heavenly

Father wants to do that much more. This is one of those truths that can sneak up on you and be a true game changer. Think about this truth for just a minute.

You may be like me and you grew up with a great dad and you see how awesome this truth really is. Maybe you are on the opposite end and you grew up with a dad who didn't invest much time in you or maybe he wasn't around for one reason or another. These verses are for you as well and perhaps even a little more meaningful. Your Heavenly Father wants (desires) to do some truly incredible things in your life. He wants to do things that only He can do. Those things are going to be unique to each person according to your needs and God's desire for you. One of the cool parts of this passage is that it tells us that these things that God wants to do in us are there for *those who ask Him*. What's stopping you? Quit reading right now and get tuned in to your Heavenly Father. Tell Him what is going on in your life. Ask Him to do in you all the things that He wants to do. It really isn't that hard. Start with *Dear God* and just go from there. Talk to Him like you are talking to your friend. Then watch and see what this Amazing God will begin to do in your life. Be careful though ... It could be a game changer for life!

CHAPTER 14

It's All about the Honor

For as long as I can remember, my dad was taking me hunting. We have hunted wild game in Louisiana, Mississippi, Alabama, Texas, Georgia, Missouri, and Wyoming. There may be more, but at this stage of the game that is all I can think of. He began taking me with him from a very early age. I remember him getting me my first Daisy BB gun and handing me my first 410 single shot. I remember the time he came home with a Remington 1100 12-gauge and told me to take care of it. I was so proud because it was just like his. I had arrived! There are so many memories that I have from the field and many of them are with him.

In 1985, my dad's company transferred him from Baton Rouge, Louisiana, to Newnan, Georgia. I wasn't particularly fond of this transition as I was in college and Baton Rouge was the place that I had called home for many years. After Dad's transfer, duck hunting took a backseat to other types of hunting due to the fact that, besides the occasional beaver pond, there just were not that many ducks in Georgia. Many people in Georgia wanted to argue that point with me; however, the numbers did not lie. Louisiana held more ducks and harvested more ducks every year than just about any other state in the country. I hated the fact that we didn't get to duck hunt much anymore. After all, what good were all those decoys if they weren't going to get used? What good was owning a pirogue (flat bottom canoe) if we were not near the marsh? It was frustrating to say the least.

After I moved to Greenville, Georgia, I began going back to Louisiana to hunt ducks several times a year. That desire began to grow in me, but I felt bad that my dad was not getting to go. In 2001, my dad helped me build my first home. As a gift to him, my wife and I presented him with a brand-new Browning shotgun dipped in camouflage and ready to hunt. With the gun, I let him know that I had set up a weekend hunt with some old friends and some new friends down south in Louisiana. The old friends were my best friend and his father, Kyle and Hershel, who lived across the street from us for years in Baton Rouge. To say the least, I think he was pretty excited.

Well, the date came and off we went. We met up with Kyle and his dad and had a great weekend with some new friends that I had gotten to know. The hunting was pretty good that weekend, but it was the least of my concerns. I got to take my dad and do for him what he had done for me many times over. That weekend hunt became an annual event as did a hunt with my dad, my son, and my nephew. I was fortunate to get into a lease situation where I have been able to take my dad several times over the last few years, and we always have a good time.

There is a lot made by people about the Ten Commandments found in the Bible. In the book of Exodus in the Old Testament these words are found: "Honor your father and your mother, so that you may live long in the land the Lord your God is giving you" (Exodus 20:12 NIV).

Interestingly enough in the New Testament these words are found in a book called Ephesians. "Honor your father and mother"—which is the first commandment with a promise—(Ephesians 6:2 NIV).

From left to right, my son, Scott; my dad, Don; and my nephew, Marc

Two different times the Bible instructs us to honor our fathers. I know that there are many ways to do that. I think for those of us who grew up hunting with our dads, taking them hunting as they age is a great way to honor them.

What ways are you honoring your father? For those of you who have lost your father, what way are you honoring his memory for your children and your grandchildren? For me, taking my dad hunting is a great way to honor who he is and what he has done in my life! How about you?

CHAPTER 15

Train 'Em Up Right!

I was thumbing through some old photo albums the other day looking at pictures of past hunts. I was amazed at how much my son had grown. I have to say it did break my heart a little. He is now a senior in high school and I couldn't be prouder of the man that he has become. I started him off duck hunting at an early age just like my father did with me. There were trips that he went on where he was not big enough to hold a gun. Then there were the trips where he was able to shoot his 20-gauge youth model and rang the ears of the people around him because of the short barrel on the gun. Then came the time when he got to shoot the big guns and hold his own in the blind. It began to get a lot more fun. Things really took a turn not long ago when he was starting to get the hang of some of the basic *quack* calls. As I or others would call, he would simply blow single note *quack* calls to go along with everyone. He enjoyed that as it added another aspect to the hunt. Then came that great moment a couple years ago. I was out of the blind working the dog on a long retrieve and some grey ducks (gadwall) started toward the blind. I was too far to hear, but I saw the birds turn and commit, and then I heard the shots ring out as I saw a couple birds fall from the sky. I was impressed.

When I got back from my walk about and settled in the blind, it was then that Scott began to tell me how he saw the birds, hollered at them with a couple calls, and then he and his friend finished off the moment by each dropping a bird. He was proud, but what he didn't know was that I was even more proud. He was turning into quite the duck hunter. I took a picture that day and posted it rather quickly on Facebook with the caption, "Train up a child in the way he should go." I liked it and so did many others. I did however wonder how many people knew where that came from.

There is a book just to the right of the middle of the Bible called Proverbs. This book is filled with wise sayings that when applied can make a huge difference in people's lives. The phrase that I referred to with the picture is actually found in chapter 22 and reads like this:

"Train up a child in the way he should go,
Even when he is old he will not depart from it."
(Proverbs 22:6 NASB)

Think about that verse for a moment. *Train up a child in the way he should go.* The implication here is that it is up to the parents, especially the father, to point their children in the right direction. This world we live in is a mixed-up, crazy kind of world. We should not think for a moment that what our kids hear at school or on TV, see on the Internet, or read on Facebook, Twitter, Instagram, or any other social media outlet is going to give them a push in the right direction. It is up to the parents to do that. There is a promise that goes along with it. *When he is old, he will not depart from it.* It does not say as he ages, as he goes through high school and thinks he knows everything, as he goes through college or the early stages of work that he won't be challenged in his beliefs. It does however say that as he gets older, as he matures, he will remember the path that he was taught to walk, and he will go that direction in life.

We only get one go-round with our kids. What are you doing to train them up in the right way? What are you doing to make sure that the right beliefs are imbedded in their minds so that when they get old they will revert back to those teachings? What are you doing to solidify those eternal truths in them so that they will be guided by those truths during the turbulent times of life? We only get one shot. Take it while they are young by teaching them the right things, the right ways, and by modeling those words with your life. When they get older, they will follow in those teachings and follow in those footsteps!

CHAPTER 16

Just Another Day
in Paradise

We had watched the weather closely, as most hunters of any kind do. We saw a front coming and with it looked like some pretty intense storms. Watching closely the night before, we decided that it looked as if there would be a small window of opportunity around daybreak and shortly thereafter, so we made the decision to head out before dawn and get set up. We were, of course, hoping all the while that we would have that opportunity that may or may not present itself. Our thought was pretty simple: we have traveled over five hundred miles and taken vacation time to be here, not to mention the season was winding down, and we had to go when we could.

We departed camp early so that we could maximize the time we thought we might have. After everything was set, we sat patiently surveying the horizon knowing what was supposed to be on the way and praying somehow that it slowed down a bit during the night. Daybreak was approaching and so was the line of clouds that were pushing from the north. We looked at our watches intently as we waited for legal shooting time. It just couldn't get there fast enough.

Within minutes of shooting time, the rain drops began to fall, the wind began to pick up, the water began to get choppy, and the atmosphere was beyond eerie. We hunkered down in the pit blind the best we could, rearranging anything we needed to keep remotely dry. There was a small roof covering over the blind, and we pushed ourselves back as far as we could get as the rain drops had now become a torrential rain. If there were any ducks that flew by, there was no way we were going to see them. I have seen some rain in my day, having grown up in Louisiana where the motto is, "If you don't like the weather, wait five minutes, it will change." This rain storm beat everything that I had ever seen before. The rain was coming down sideways out of the north and blowing straight into the blind as we sat facing north. *Miserable* is not even a word that came close to describing what this storm was making us. The winds were literally howling. There was lightning and thunder popping all around us. We actually heard later that there were tornadoes not far from where we were. Just when I thought I couldn't stand any more, I looked off the right end of the blind and there on the outskirts of the decoys sat a small group of what I grew up calling blackjacks. A group of ring-necks had flown through this storm and lit just outside the decoy spread. In the midst of that storm, I told the guys to get ready, there were ducks out there!

There is a very similar story found in the book of Matthew in the Bible. Chapter 14 tells a story of a group of guys known as the disciples of Jesus who were caught in a huge storm in their boat on a place called the Sea of Galilee. The winds, waves, and rain were so intense that these experienced fishermen were literally fearful for their lives. As all of this was taking place, they saw something moving toward them and thought it to be a ghost. Now really afraid, they cried out in fear. Jesus, as He approached the boat walking on the water, told them not to be afraid and assured them that it was He so that they would calm down. Not being able to see him, a guy named Peter began to call back to Jesus and asked

Him to give the go-ahead to come out and meet him if it was truly Him. Jesus gave the go-ahead, and Peter got out of the boat and actually walked on the water. There is an interesting occurrence in verses 30 and 31 as it states, "But when he saw the wind, he was afraid and, beginning to sink, cried out, 'Lord, save me!' Immediately Jesus reached out his hand and caught him. 'You of little faith' he said, 'why did you doubt?'" (Matthew 14:30, 31 NIV). Peter saw the winds and began to sink, but Jesus reached out His hand and picked him back up.

There are a couple parts of this that really hit home for us. In the middle of life's storms, it is so easy to concentrate on the winds swirling around us. To see our circumstances is quite often the first thing that we do. The problem with concentrating on our circumstances is that in doing so we take our focus off Jesus, who is the one who helps us through these storms. When Peter took his eyes off Jesus, he began to sink. The same thing happens to us. We find ourselves sinking in the middle of life's storms when we lose focus on what really matters the most.

The other aspect of this is that when Peter began to sink and cried out to Jesus, He (Jesus) took Peter by the hand and picked him back up and guided him safely through the storm. There are so many people I know that, as I write this, are trying to get through storms that are raging all around them—storms that are fierce like cancer storms, marital storms, financial storms, and many others. The only way that we can navigate through these storms and come out safely on the other side is to reach up and take the hand of Jesus and let Him guide us through what we are going through. The greatness of the story is that it teaches us that Jesus responded immediately to Peter, and He responds to us the exact same way. He has His hand extended your way right now in an attempt to help you. Will you reach up and grab His hand, so to speak? Ask Him to help you navigate through whatever you might be facing and I promise you, He will respond.

Look out through the storm; you might just see something you like.

CHAPTER 17

Don't Worry, Son!

I don't know how many of you have ever heard of a nutria before. A nutria is an overgrown rat that terrorizes the marshes of south Louisiana and the young boys that go there. Nutria have been a problem for years in the coastal areas of south Louisiana due to the fact that they eat much of the vegetation that grows in the marshes. When that vegetation begins to disappear, the Gulf waters make their way inland and the marshes begin to diminish and the coastline begins to disappear. I realize that I oversimplified all that is happening with the marshes and the coastline. Furthermore, I realize that I placed the major bulk of the problem squarely on the back of that pesky marsh rodent. Don't worry, the nutria deserve it. I never have liked them anyway.

When I was a young boy, there was an old trapper named Jim who lived way back in the swamp and trapped nutria as well as other things for a living. Jim was an interesting guy who I will talk about in another chapter of the book. He was pretty good at what he did, I guess, because every time I came out of the march from duck hunting, Trapper Jim had nutria pelts hanging on the line drying out. Jim would place his traps all over the place in the hopes of catching as many as he could.

One particular morning, my dad and I were loaded up in the pirogue and headed for the duck blind. I was in the front, with my poor dad push poling in the back. I was probably only six or seven years old at the time. I was too young to have my own pirogue. As we rounded a bend, I came face to face with a trapped nutria. This baby was huge. It had to be the biggest in the marsh, or so my young mind thought. I was scared to death. He started to thrash around. I had no idea he was trapped already. In my mind, he was coming in the boat and was going to do some damage to me. As I showed my fear, I will never forget my dad telling me not to worry, that rat couldn't hurt me. I was perfectly safe with him. Those words echoed in my mind for years and still do today at many times in life.

They remind me that not only was I safe in the presence of my father then, but also that I am safe in the presence of my Heavenly Father now. A guy named Paul wrote these words, recorded in letter written to the church at Corinth. This letter is found in the New Testament of the Bible in 1 Corinthians: "Grace and peace to you from God our Father and the Lord Jesus Christ" (1 Corinthians 1:3 NIV).

This verse reminds me that my life ought to be characterized by not only grace, but peace as well. God wants us to have peace in our lives. He doesn't want us to be consumed with things like fear, doubt, anxiety, worry, stress, as well as a host of other things that can detract from our lives. As men, we never really like to admit that some of these things are in our lives. It makes us feel weak somehow. The fact of the matter is that these things do come into our lives when we least expect them. When my son was born early and his oxygen level wasn't right, I was scared. There wasn't anything that I could do but pray and let the peace of God cover me. When my job wasn't going well and I thought I might lose it, all I could do was ask God for His peace to invade my life. When our finances got tight, and the stress of that weight began to take its toll, my only recourse was to ask for God's peace to take control and relieve me of this burden. In all those cases and a million more, God has always given me His peace to let me know that things would work out if

I would trust Him. I still have my moments, as I expect you do as well. When those times hit, join me in asking God for His peace to take root in our lives and do in us more than we could ever imagine possible. It does work, I promise. Now ask Him for that peace that you are looking for and experience it for yourself. It is incredible to say the least.

CHAPTER 18

Did You See That Hit?

The setting was much the same as many that I have been speaking of already in this book. My dad and I were west of Lafayette, Louisiana, hunting in a pit blind in the middle of some flooded agricultural fields. The ducks and the geese were flying pretty good, and we were having a good hunt. I don't remember who shot this particular bird, although because it was only winged, it more than likely was me due to the fact that Dad was a much better shot than I was. Having said that, this specklebelly goose went down like a 747 going down over New Orleans International Airport. He had his own runway, I believe. Being the younger one, I took the dog that we owned for a few years now and began the slow trudge across the gumbo mud field toward the bird that was easily three to four hundred yards away. We closed the distance, and I was able to send the dog after the bird. However, when the dog got close, this bird got angry and protective. The bird stood up, cupped its wings, crooked its neck, and hissed at the dog. This dog of ours stopped and looked back at me as if to say, "What do I do now?" I give the *fetch it up* command but to no avail. I had to go take a finishing shot from a ways off, as the goose had begun walking away from me. Then and only then did this dog make the retrieve. I relayed this story to my father as

Beyond the Blind

I got back in the blind, catching my breath as I recapped the events. He let me know of his continued disappointment in this dog and that he was selling him soon.

As the story goes, we sold this dog due to poor performance in the field and bought a new pup after the season and began training him for the next season. This new dog, Gator, progressed nicely, and we had high expectations for him.

Fast forward a few months to the same place in the same blind with the same scenario. A goose gets shot and sails, and Gator and I go *en route* to retrieve this bird. As we get about one hundred yards away or so, I send Gator back on this bird, and this ten month old takes off like I lit a firecracker near him. As he approached this bird, it does what the other bird did, almost exactly. As this bird prepares to defend itself, something I will never forget happened. Gator, going full stride, never slowed down as the bird stood, cupped, crooked, and hissed. Gator hit him like a linebacker in Tiger Stadium on a Saturday night. The bird turned a somersault backward, and before it knew what hit it, Gator had a paw on its neck and picked him up with his mouth and brought him back with his first goose retrieval. He was proud. I was proud. I knew Dad was going to be proud. That dog showed no fear whatsoever. As I relayed the story to my dad, all I could say was, "We got ourselves a dog!"

As I think about that moment, I also think about a verse in the Bible where a guy named Paul wrote to a guy named Timothy. Paul was older and more experienced in preaching and other things while Timothy was a younger, less experienced guy. Paul told Him, "For God has not given us a spirit of fearfulness, but one of power, love, and sound judgment" (2 Timothy 1:7 HCSB).

God has not given us a spirit of fear. Paul was encouraging Timothy to do what he was called to do and to go about those things without fear, but to know that he had been given the power to accomplish those things by God. The same is true for us today. God has not given us a spirit of fear, and yet fear holds us back from doing many things in life. At times, we find ourselves paralyzed by fear of failure, fear of the unknown, fear of humiliation, fear of not having the answers as well as a host of other fears. God has instead given us power that comes from His presence in our lives. He has given us the capacity to love and be loved by Him. He has given us a mind that can lead us into some incredible moments that He has in store for us. What is it that God may be leading you to do in your life? What is it that is or has been holding you back? Never forget that a spirit of fear is not something that God has placed in you. Get rid of that fear and approach your opportunities with confidence and with power, knowing that God is working in you and through you as you trust and follow Him. When you begin to do this, be prepared—your life just might never be the same again.

CHAPTER 19

The Value of Patience

E very outdoor enthusiast has a goal in mind. For the deer hunter, it is that first buck, then that eight-point buck, then ultimately it is that Boone and Crockett buck that everyone hears about for ages. For the turkey hunter, it is the grand slam, and for the duck hunter it is the banded bird. It is the ultimate prize for the waterfowler. I had been around several people who got banded birds. My dad got one when I was young on a trip that my sister got to go on. (I won't vent about that now.) I was with my buddy when he got his first band on the opposite end of the blind from me. I got to hold the one my dad got on a farm pond where they were shooting Canadian geese, and I was a part of one where I was sure the bird picked up was the one I shot that had a band on it. It was a greenhead, and it was right where I thought it should be as it went down a little ways off, but when you are hunting in a blind with six other people, someone else ended up with it. Oh, well, what are you going to do except be happy for that person?

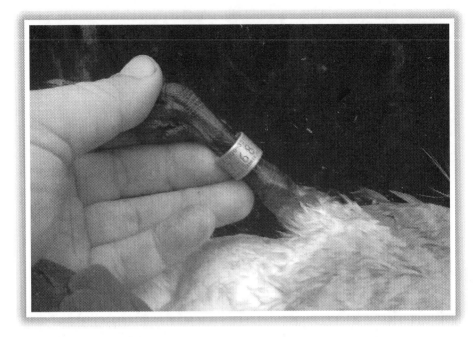

Then my time came, and I will never forget it. A lone lesser Canadian came by the blind, gave us a look, and moved on. I was up looking and kept my eye on the bird as it flew a long ways off and then made a circle and headed back our way. To make a long story short, the bird came back on the backside of the blind and closed the distance to about ten yards. As the bird fell, I jumped out of the blind; my buddy's dog made the easy retrieve and brought the bird to my hand. There it was! Much to my surprise as I looked at the leg, there was the elusive band.

The journey was over, the band was in hand, and the ultimate prize was taken. I was happy to say the least. It took some time, as every hunter knows, but it was well worth the wait.

There is a verse in the New Testament of the Bible found in Hebrews that says, "When God made his promise to Abraham, since there was no one greater for him to swear by, he swore by himself, saying, 'I will surely bless you and give you many descendants.' And so after waiting patiently, Abraham received what was promised" (Hebrews 6:13–15 NIV).

Beyond the Blind

When life gets tough, our patience tends to get thin. It is in these times that we have to be more patient than ever and trust that God is in control. Through the last twenty-five years, I have been a part of many people's lives when they were walking through the toughest times they had ever seen. It was so easy to give up and let go of things. Part of what I get to do is remind them that God's promises to them are valid and true, and if they will be patient they will see those promises come to pass before their very eyes.

I don't know what you are facing in your life right now, but I do know that life can be tough. Things don't work out the way we dreamed they would. People are always letting us down. Circumstances are cruel to every person at certain times. There is no way around these things. I also know that God has a plan and His timing is perfect. It is hard to see that and may be much harder to believe it sometimes, but it is still true. If you will be patient, God will work in your life and do things that only He can do. You have to believe that! For when we are patient and wait for God to do His thing, it is always better than what we had planned or what we envisioned. Be patient and let God do His thing. You will never regret that move.

CHAPTER 20

Divine Appointments

E very year my friends and I take a couple trips from Georgia to Jones, Louisiana, to hunt at Megabucks Duck Lodge with guide and friend Johnny Wink. My longtime friend from Baton Rouge usually meets us there for what has become one of our annual get-togethers. If memory serves me right, we have been going there now for thirteen or fourteen years, and it is one of the trips that I look forward to as much or more than any trip I take. Johnny Wink is the owner and operator of Megabucks, and there really are very few words to describe him. He is one of a kind. If you don't believe me, just ask him. He will tell you the same.

A couple of years ago I was traveling out on Sunday night after I finished my responsibilities at church and was to join up with the group for a few days of hunting at the start of the second split. I was in a hurry to get there as I had gotten two days of reports from the rest of my group telling me that the hunting had been phenomenal. Those kinds of reports always make the drive much more bearable … not to mention, I was looking forward to a few days off. Don't get me wrong, I love what I do. However, those who are on call twenty-four hours a day look forward to a break anytime they can get it, and I am no exception to the rule. I made the trek and got into camp around midnight or a little later. I went ahead and got all my stuff ready to roll for the morning hunt just to make sure that I didn't forget anything. Everything was set, and I eagerly went to bed anticipating a great hunt in the morning.

As I previously mentioned, Johnny Wink is one of a kind and is notorious for waking up everyone in the camp between 4:00 a.m. and 4:30 a.m. with a loud shout of *hooty hoo!* We are not sure where *hooty hoo* came from, and quite frankly I am not sure of the spelling. All I know is that I have heard it on many occasions before my alarm had a chance to sound off. On this morning I do not remember hearing the strange call, but I was awakened by my buddy Chuck. As I stumbled out of bed with little sleep, I noticed Johnny sitting out on his back porch in a rocking chair looking very subdued. Chuck soon informed me that Johnny had just received a call that his father had passed away. Well, it looked like things just turned on a moment's notice. Johnny was not expecting that call, and I was not expecting to work. However, in no way was I going to pass up the chance to help Johnny out in his time of crisis. We talked that morning before the hunt and even during the hunt. There was nothing that he could do at the moment since his family was having to travel to Monroe, Louisiana, so we went on the morning hunt. We hunted, laughed, talked about his dad some, told stories, and in general had a good time together in the midst of a bad moment. As we returned, I talked Johnny through what he needed at the funeral home, what they were going to talk with him about, who he needed to contact, and other details pertaining to all that would be necessary for him to do.

As I think back on that whole experience and the days that we were there, I ask myself this question: What are the chances that a minister would arrive at the duck camp the same night that the guide's dad would die? As I answer that question, I am reminded of a really insightful verse found in Ephesians: "For we are God's handiwork, created in Christ Jesus to do good works, which God prepared in advance for us to do" (Ephesians 2:10 NIV).

The entire verse speaks volumes. We are God's handiwork. Some translations use the word *workmanship*. This word means that we are God's work of art or, simply put, we are His masterpiece. He uniquely made us and gave each of us certain qualities and gifts to be used by Him and for Him. The verse goes on from there, now doesn't it? It goes on to say that these good works were "prepared in advance for us to do." What are the chances that I would be there on the day that Johnny would need a preacher hanging around? Maybe some people would answer with the old *slim-to-none* response, but I would say that I was there because it was a work that God had prepared in advance for me to be a part of. I don't think things happen randomly. I believe that God has what I call *divine appointments* for each of us so that we can be instrumental in making a difference in the lives of the people that we are around and even in the lives of people that we randomly bump into.

Think about that truth for a minute and let it sink in. You were created by God to do great things and to make a difference in the lives of the people you encounter. What an awesome thought that is and one that, when grabbed hold of, may actually alter your life from now on. I know it has altered my life. How about you? Are you ready to step up? I hope so, because once you realize that you are God's handiwork, you will never be the same again.

CHAPTER 21

You Better Stop That!

I have been through a few retrievers in my time. My dad and I had a few; the best dog was named Gator. I have had a few as an adult that have been good and bad. I had one I trained that was very good while I had one that I sent off that got ruined by a trainer. I had another that I thought was going to be good and didn't turn out well. Having gone through a run of bad luck over a few years with training, trainers, poor instincts, and one that got hit by a car, I was disappointed to say the least. I just wanted a good dog that could hunt with me.

I heard through a friend that there was a dog at a hunt test that was jam-up and for sale. I went to look at this dog and saw what he was doing and was capable of doing, and I took one last chance to see what would happen. This dog's name was Bolo, which I wasn't crazy about until I learned that it was a term that stood for *Be on the Lookout.* Then for a retriever, I thought that the name was pretty cool. Bolo and I worked hard, and he was ready for hunting season. I'm not going to lie, we had a great season but still had some things to learn. He really did do well, but I also saw some things that we needed to fine tune in the off season. We once again worked hard, and he improved nicely in preparation for his second season. I was thrilled with his progress and very excited about what he would do.

Beyond the Blind

On one of his first hunts, he did not let me down. He did everything I wanted him to do and more. He performed like a champ. Then we got to the second day. He did well, but there was an incident, something I saw that I didn't like very much at all. Here is the story. We had several people hunting out of a large pit blind in North Louisiana. We had a great volley at a large flock of ducks and dropped multiple birds. My buddy Chuck worked his new dog on his end while I worked Bolo on my end. Bolo and I went after several ducks. He brought the first one back perfectly, and I promptly sent him back on the second. That's when it happened. There were literally three ducks in a row. Now it was not uncommon for him to bring in two at a time if and when he could manage them, but this time he looked over and saw his partner heading his way to help out, and he didn't like it one bit. He began to try to herd all three together without bringing one in first. I called and whistled and called again, but he would have nothing to do with it. He wanted all three. Finally, after I reached a level beyond frustration, he brought back one, thinking he could go back after the other two. By this time though, Chuck and his dog Addie were with us, and Bolo had to sit and watch Addie get the other two. He didn't like that very much, but that was his punishment for being selfish.

In the New Testament of the Bible in a book called Philippians, there is a verse that addresses the sin problem that plagues so many of us. It says, "Do nothing out of selfish ambition or vain conceit. Rather, in humility value others above yourselves" (Philippians 2:3 NIV). We are to do nothing out of our own selfish ambition. That was hard for Bolo to do that day. Addie was coming, and he wanted to do it all by himself. (Or maybe he was showing off for the new girl.) Many men are like this in so many ways. We want things for ourselves, or we want things our way. Bolo had a point, I'm sure, if he could have just communicated that to me. He had worked hard. He had endured much. He had trained diligently. He had put in his time. He deserved to get all those birds. After all, they were on his end of the blind. That was only fair! Sounds like a lot of the people that I talk to and even some of the conversations that I have with myself. It is part of our human nature to be selfish, and that is why this verse is there for us to read and why it is so important for us to understand it and apply it to our lives. God wants us to value those around us and desire great things to happen in their lives. He wants us to consider others as more important than ourselves. What would happen if we thought of our wives as more important that ourselves? What about thinking this way about our friends? You get the point. If we began to see others as more important than ourselves, it would place a new value on those people who are around us every day.

Bolo learned a lesson that day that he will remember. I wonder how many of us will learn that same lesson. Don't do anything that has a selfish motive! Novel idea, don't you think? Consider those around you as more important than yourself, and in doing so you might just amaze those people and transform those relationships into something you hold tightly for the rest of your life. Just a thought.

CHAPTER 22

What to Do? What to Do?

I t was one of those days that we all have. In fact it was one of those trips that we all dread, but we know that it is going to happen sooner or later. Everything seems to be perfect, but the action just isn't there. This was the case for this trip several years ago.

My buddies and I made our plans to meet up for a mid-January hunt. We worked on the calendar to make sure that everything was going to work out for each of the guys involved. After much planning, the dates were set, and everyone was pumped up about the hunt.

The day arrived for us to leave, and we made the trip with great anticipation. We looked forward to a great time and a great hunt. It never really matters about the number of ducks we get. What does matter is that we all get to enjoy a getaway from the pressures associated with our jobs and our day-to-day responsibilities. We get to enjoy friendships that have been part of our lives for many years, some going back into my childhood days. We met at camp that night, enjoyed some good food, and shot the breeze a little bit about what had been going on in our lives. Those are good times and what so many of my memories are made of. We were there for three days and knew that we would have a lot more time to talk, so we called it a night and hit the sack.

The next morning was perfect. The temperature hovered around the freezing mark. The sky was breaking with very few clouds in sight. It was going to be a bluebird kind of day with the sun reflecting off the spinning wings of the Mojo mallard decoys. We started off great with a few birds at daybreak, but then it seemed to slow down rather quickly. We picked up a few more as the morning went along but would not call the day an overwhelming success from a hunting standpoint. Day two was almost identical but with a few less ducks both sighted and killed. The weather remained beautiful, but the hunting just wasn't right.

As we contemplated our third and final day, we decided to move to another location in hopes of mixing things up a bit. We took off that morning cautiously optimistic about what the day would hold. Before legal shooting time arrived, several of us stood and watched, hoping to see some movement or hear the whistling of wings coming by. Our efforts produced nothing. As the hunt began, we were not seeing anything, much less getting the opportunity to call anything toward us. I know since you are reading this book that you are thinking the switch got turned on and the barrels got hot from all the shooting. Sorry to disappoint you, but nothing even close to that happened. In fact, we sat in frustration for about an hour and literally saw only a few birds in the distance. As I looked at the guys, we all had the same thought. Let's get the heck out of Dodge. We had an eight-hour drive ahead of us, and we were convinced that nothing was going to change. Why waste any more time? We packed it in and headed home. We had a great time but a poor hunt. We needed to use our time to our benefit for the ride home.

Using our time wisely is actually a Biblical teaching that many people tend to overlook. In the book of Ephesians in the New Testament, there are these words recorded for us in chapter 5: "Be very careful, then, how you live—not as unwise but as wise, making the most of every opportunity, because the days are evil" (Ephesians 5:15, 16 NIV).

We are instructed to live wisely in the world and to make the most of the time that God has given to us. That means that we have to make careful and wise choices. This involves our time at work, at home, socially, recreationally, and yes, even at church. The question that we must ask ourselves when it comes to our choices and the way that we spend our time is the question, "Is this wise?" Is it wise to work so many hours that we offer our children on the altar of success? Is it wise to spend too much time recreationally at the expense of our marriage? Is it wise to be slack when it comes to our professional work ethic and sacrifice our job, thus not being able to support our family?

These are tough questions, and there is a fine line to the answer to each of them. We need the wisdom of God to guide us in using our time wisely for the benefit of those people around us and for ourselves. If this is something you are struggling with, I recommend a book to help you titled *Choosing to Cheat*. Author and pastor Andy Stanley does a great job breaking down these areas that are necessary for each of us, especially men, and to direct us to make the wise decisions that directly impact our lives. Using our time wisely by asking that important question, "Is this wise?" may be one of the most important and transforming steps you will ever take. Ask yourself this question as you examine your life. When you do, be prepared to make some adjustments to keep the different aspects of your life prioritized correctly. When you do, life just might take an unexpected turn that you will really like!

CHAPTER 23

I Got Ya Now

The hunt was amazing, the weather was awful, and the day was taking a turn for the worst. I was in North Louisiana with some really good friends hunting several years ago. The temperatures had dropped below freezing, and the sleet was coming down, but the hunting had been fantastic. We had a mixed bag of mallards, gadwall, and pintails. We were a few ducks shy of the limit, but the weather was getting worse and we had an elderly man with us, so we made the call to head out. We knew that we had a couple of miles to ride out on the four-wheeler, and we had to tag team getting the group out. It was an easy call to make on who went first. We let my buddy Chuck and his father, Papa T, go out first so Papa T could get in the vehicle and get some heat going. They took off and we waited.

As the four-wheeler arrived to get the next two, we were informed that we needed to make sure that we had everything in order as far as our licenses and IDs due to the fact that there was a federal game warden at our truck checking everything down to the last detail. I knew all my stuff was in order, so I grabbed my stuff and took off for the truck. Upon arrival I showed the young warden everything he needed to see and showed him the ducks that I had shot. As I took my ducks from the pile of ducks and showed him, he immediately threw them back in the pile and waited. As the last of the group arrived, he went through the same thing with them and then told us that he was going to have to write us all tickets for illegal transportation of game. Needless to say, no one was happy about this decision on his part, and I'm sure we made our displeasure very obvious. As the warden and I talked, he explained to me what we had done wrong. In our haste to leave the blind, we all put our ducks in the basket on the front of the four-wheeler, thus not maintaining our possession of them. By the letter of the law, he had us. He was right, we were wrong. I explained to him that it was indeed an honest mistake and careless on our part, but we were in a hurry to get a very cold, elderly man into some heat, and we just didn't think about that aspect of what we were doing. He went to his truck and radioed his supervisor and informed him of what was going on. I heard his supervisor ask him a series of questions: "Are they over the limit?" "Do they each have a license?" "Are their shotguns and shells legal?" The answer was *yes* to each question. Then he said, "Well, tell them what they did wrong. Warn them and let them go." I was relieved to hear that statement. We got off with a warning and were very grateful for that.

The problem that I had that day was that as a minister and as a Christian man I knew that the Bible taught me to "be above reproach" (1 Timothy 3:2 NIV).

Not knowing the law or not thinking about the law was no excuse for me. I needed to live my life as an example to those around me. This is really true for all of us. As Christian men, we need to be the ones out there setting the example. I'm not talking here about alienating all your hunting buddies by taking the *holier than thou* approach or the *I'm better than you* approach. I am however advocating setting an example for anyone who is watching your actions so that they may follow that example if they so choose. I know that I have had the opportunity through the years to set good examples, and I'm sure that at times I have faltered in that very same attempt. All I can do is give God my best and ask Him to help me when I need it. I always have to remember that it doesn't matter if the other guys around me are watching me or not; I have one set of eyes on me most of the time, and those eyes belong to my son. I know he is watching me and following my every move. I am reminded of a great country song that came out a few years ago titled "Watching You" by Rodney Atkins. The chorus of the song says this:

He said, "I've been watching you, Dad, ain't that cool?

I'm your buckaroo, I wanna be like you.

And eat all my food and grow as tall as you are.

We got cowboy boots and camo pants

Yeah, we're just alike, hey, ain't we, Dad?

I want to do everything you do.

So I've been watching you."

With eyes watching me by my son and others, I do my very best to live *above reproach* so that those around me may see what authentic Christian living is all about. The cool thing is that in doing so, my life not only becomes a blessing for others, but I am blessed at the same time.

By the way, there are now at least three or four extra game carriers in my blind bag just in case someone with the group doesn't have one. I'm not getting in that mess again!

CHAPTER 24

Tell Me about It!

There is a place that I have been going now for a little over ten years that I look forward to every year. Opening day of the Louisiana duck season, I will usually be found in central Louisiana with my dad; my great friend from childhood, Kyle; his father; and some newer friends that I have had the privilege of getting to know over the years. The hunting is on private land that is managed intensely for ducks and deer. The duck hunting is usually phenomenal, and the deer hunting potential is incredible. There is also a more than average chance to shoot a hog or two, and it is greatly encouraged so as to get rid of as many of those beasts as possible.

One of the cool things about the length of time I have been hunting there is seeing the progress that has taken place as this property has been carefully and specifically developed. Besides the improvements on the hunting side of things, there have also been other developments around camp. They have built a huge fire pit that is usually roaring as we come in from the evening deer hunt. There are rocking chairs surrounding the pit, and it is a great place to sit and share the stories from the days' hunts. The last couple of years, they have also added a large projection screen that has been set up to view the Louisiana State University football games. I can hardly picture anything better than this. I am sitting with my dad and fantastic friends, eating and talking about the hunt, and watching LSU football. Life is good! These moments that we have together are some of my all-time favorites. Getting to share these memories with a bunch of guys that I am so close to is priceless. You know the moments that I am talking about. They happen at hunting camps across this nation every fall with guys just like the ones I am talking about. Fathers sit talking to their sons about life while others sit and share those moments where you laugh so hard you think your sides are going to pop open. These moments are what make life more bearable, and they are the moments that God gave to us to take the edge off.

The Old Testament book of Proverbs has many wise things to say. The writer says this in chapter 17:

> A friend loves at all times,
> and a brother is born for a time of adversity."
> (Proverbs 17:17 NIV)

It really is nice to know who your real friends are. Everyone needs good friends. I can honestly say that I have been blessed with some of the best friends a man could ever have. My friends have brought me laughter in life's finest moments. They have picked me up in some of life's darkest moments. They have encouraged me in life's most frustrating moments. They have been there every step of the way.

There is a great country song that I thought of sung by Tracy Lawrence called "Find Out Who Your Friends Are." Part of the song goes like this:

Run your car off the side of the road,
Get stuck in a ditch way out in the middle of nowhere,
Or get yourself in a bind, lose the shirt off your back …
You find out who your friends are.

—"Find Out Who Your Friends Are," songwriters:
Edward Hill, Casey Beathard

The songwriter goes on to paint a beautiful word picture of someone who will drop everything that he or she is doing to come lend a hand, no matter where you are or what kind of bind you might find yourself in. These true friends are the ones who don't consider the cost or the time required to help; they see you above everything else and come running to help out. I'm sure you can hear this song on YouTube if you have never heard it before.

We need to stop and realize that God places friends in our lives who meet some of our deepest needs. These friends are gifts. They are there for a reason and a purpose. The times that we have to sit around that campfire, to share a meal and a story, to catch up with all the things that have been going on, those are the times we will never forget. Those are the times we can really be ourselves. We are transparent to our friends. They know what we are thinking before we can verbalize it. They read our body language and know when something is wrong. They hear concern or anxiety in our voices. They know us almost as well as we know ourselves.

Spend some time today thanking God for those friends that He has placed in your life. Spend some time reflecting on some of those great times. Send a quick email, and set up a hunt, and get together with those guys that bring meaning to your life. They are part of God's provision for you. Enjoy the moments. God gives them to you for a reason!

CHAPTER 25

Whatcha Got?

One thing I have learned, especially since the majority of my hunting is out of state, is to make sure that there are extras of just about everything. If you look in my blind bag, for example, there are many things that I don't normally use, but I am glad these things are there. There are extra game carriers, extra duck calls, an extra goose call, extra reeds for the calls I use, as well as an extra box of shells or two. At certain places that we go in certain blinds, we will have an extra gun or two in the blind just in case. On more than one occasion, someone has needed the extra gun due to a broken part or a jam that was just nasty. We have been down to the wire where we are grabbing shells from anyone who has any left. Don't even get me started about the snack wagon or the snack bag. There is no claiming beforehand what is yours and what is someone else's.

Everything is up for grabs to the first one who can grab it, so get what you want when you can get your hands on it. It is basically a share-and-share-alike mentality.

This is the same mentality that those who were a part of the early church had in their lives. In the fifth book of the New Testament, the book of Acts, there is a description of these very interesting people that tells us: "All the believers were together and had everything in common. They sold property and possessions to give to anyone who had need. Every day they continued to meet together in the temple courts. They broke bread in their homes and ate together with glad and sincere hearts" (Acts 2:44–46 NIV).

These people who made up the early church understood that things happen in life and that there are moments when we have what someone else needs to get by or maybe even succeed. I am not talking about the swindlers on the street, but rather those that you are around daily. Those people who are in your circle of influence may actually be the ones who need something from you. It may be that they need something in the way of material possessions. It may be that they simply need a word of encouragement. It is up to you to look around and see those people and what they may be in need of. When you identify them and their need, see if there is any way that you can help. There are times when I was not in a position to help out, but I was able to network to find the help that they needed. There are so many ways to help people, and in today's times, there seem to be more and more opportunities to do some great things for those around you. Take a moment and look around. What do you see? How can you help? What can you do? Take that opportunity to bless someone near you. You will thank me later for the feeling that comes with doing something great for someone else. That's just the way it works. Try it! You will like it!

CHAPTER 26

You Have Got to Be Kidding Me!

As my kids have gotten older and more involved in sports and the social scene, they have needed a little less of my time. Don't get me wrong; I miss coaching their teams year-round and being at every event known to mankind. However, there has been an upside. I get to hunt more than I have in years. That I like! A couple years ago I put together a five-day trip for myself and one of my good friends from town. We had been hunting together now for twelve or thirteen years, mostly on trips that he had put together. This was my turn to organize the trip and, in a way, pay him back a little for all the effort he had put in over the years. We were headed to North Louisiana for three days and then hopping down to south Louisiana for two days before heading home. I was more than excited about this trip. We were hunting with some longtime friends up north, and I was going to have the chance to introduce him to some of my friends in south Louisiana that I had gotten to know recently through some hunts that I had been on.

The first three days of our hunt were met with some crazy weather as an arctic blast moved across the state. We had everything from rain, to sleet, to snow, with freezing temperatures along the way. The hunting was hit-and-miss but overall a very good hunt and a great time. After day three up north, we packed the trailer and headed south. I was pretty excited to get down south and introduce Chuck around to some new guys and a new hunting location that he had not been to before.

As we arrived in south Louisiana, so did the frontal system. Temperatures dropped to near record lows. The rice fields, being shallow already, froze solid in a small amount of time. As we arrived at the blind for day four of our hunt, we realized that we had our work cut out for us from the beginning. I used the four-wheeler to break up ice, moved a few decoys around, got the heaters working so as not to be too miserable as we waited the arrival of our green-headed friends with bright orange feet. We were hunting with another good friend of mine from the Baton Rouge area, and I was glad to get these two guys together. Daybreak came and went with no action whatsoever. The later in the morning it got, the more frustrated I became. I wanted everything to go just right, and this weather had messed everything up. We literally saw one duck the entire morning, and that bird was in the stratosphere. Can you say the trip was a *bust*? The ducks had pushed into the marsh and were nowhere near us. Knowing the weather was going to be the same the next day, we made the call and headed home. Disappointed would not even begin to describe how I felt.

Found right in the middle of the Bible, the writer of Psalms 42 writes these words:

"Why, my soul, are you downcast?
Why so disturbed within me?
Put your hope in God,
for I will yet praise Him,
my Savior and my God." (Psalm 42:11 NIV)

As I read these words, I am keenly aware of the fact that life is full of disappointments. Life has always been this way, is that way right now, and will always be this way. There is hardly a day that goes by, much less a week, where life doesn't hand us disappointments. It is in these times that we tend to lose our way. We lose our focus on God. We slip into a sense of anxiety, frustration, or even worse, depression. We frantically try to find a quick fix. We look for a solution that seems to elude us. Many times after all these attempts have been made, along with many more, we give up.

Giving up is, to me, never an option. God has a better plan and greater solutions than we can ever imagine. That is why the writer of this Psalm begs us, implores us, and commands us to *put our hope in God*. This is what every single one of us needs to do, and yet very few of us will actually do it. We are trained to think differently but hardwired to trust. Our life experiences have many times made us individuals who are skeptical and don't trust very easily. The fact of the matter is that God wants us, desires for us, to trust Him. We need to remember that the God who created all that we get to see in the outdoors as sportsmen is the same God who is working in our lives every day. Look around and you will see His handiwork. Look within and you will see the same! Place your hope in Him and He will never let you down!

CHAPTER 27

It's NASCAR, Baby!

The week leading up to the hunting trip had been a hectic week to say the least. There had been so many different things pop up that I had to take care of that I really thought I was going to lose my mind. When life gets that crazy for me, I get very list driven. I had hospital visits to make, a funeral to take care of, Bible studies to prep for, and a trip to pack for with many different things that had to be done to get ready to leave in just a few days. The list was written, but it seemed that each time I crossed something off the list, I added something else to take its place.

Well, everything that could get done, got done. That's my story and I'm sticking to it. We were taking my friend Chuck's youngest son and one of his best friends as well as a dog, all our supplies, and two four-wheelers on my trailer. Chuck came over and we loaded everything up, got the four-wheelers on the trailer, and got everything strapped down. I knew that I was forgetting to do something, but for the life of me, I couldn't remember what it was, so off we went. The guys got settled in, and of course were asleep before we got far. This may have been the only time that I was looking forward to an eight-hour ride in the car. I was exhausted, and just sitting and resting while visiting with some good friends sounded rather refreshing to say the least.

The trip was going without complication. Another friend from Atlanta was traveling ahead of us and called several times to give us the *all-clear* report. It seemed that the trip would be uneventful as most of our trips had been for years. Man, can things turn in a moment without warning. As I pulled out my pillow and propped it against the window to get a quick nap, I heard a loud booming sound and felt a jerk on the truck. I sat up quickly and looked behind us to see the trailer spitting out sparks everywhere and one of the tires bouncing across both lanes of traffic on I-20 heading toward the median. As I watched in horror and complete disgust, one of the guys from the back yells out, "Looks just like NASCAR!" As it turned out, the one thing that I forgot not only to put on my list, but also to actually do was grease the axle before we left. I had neglected proper maintenance, and it was now costing us dearly.

We enacted a plan to get things taken care of, which included two guys staying with the trailer and gear while the other two went looking for some help. We found a place just up the road that could help. They hauled the trailer to the shop. We went on a three-hour round trip to get a new axle from the closest dealer. When we got the axle back and installed, the man told me he only accepted cash. No checks. No credit cards. The bill was over $400. I spent everything that I had, and I hadn't even made it to camp yet. Talk about starting a trip off on the wrong foot. I had done it. It was all because I neglected the important things that should have been done. I knew what to do, and I knew how to do it. I even had everything at the house to take care of the situation. I just didn't do it.

There is a verse in the New Testament in the book of James that says, "If anyone, then, knows the good they ought to do and doesn't do it, it is sin for them" (James 4:17 NIV). James is reminding us that there are certain things in life that we are not only supposed to do, but we are actually meant to do. God gives us awesome opportunities to do some incredible things. There are so many circumstances that come our way every day where God wants us to step up and do those things He places before us. In the same way, there are many times when we fail to act upon those opportunities. There are other times when we fail to even recognize these incredible moments.

God not only wants to live in our lives, He wants to live through our lives. This is not that farfetched an idea, and it doesn't require you to move to a distant country to do something that you feel you are not equipped to do. Many times the way that God wants to work through you may be right there in your family. There are other times where He wants to work through you where you work. There are other times where He might just drop an opportunity in your lap to do a good deed, a great work, or just do the right thing when no one else is looking. When these moments come, we need to be prepared to seize those moments. James reminds us that for those of us who know the right thing to do and we fail to do it, to us it is sin.

We need to get to the point in our lives where we no longer miss those moments. We need to be keenly aware of what God is doing around us so that we can recognize what He wants to do through us. I know for me, I now understand the right things to do, I know how to do those things, and I am equipped by God to do whatever it is that God leads me to do. Now it is up to me to do these things. The same is true for you. God has given you certain talents, and He wants you to use them to do good things as He presents those opportunities to you. You are going to have to trust me on this—these are the moments that will define you as you move forward in your walk with God. When you see these moments, seize them! These moments are life changing, life altering moments that you will remember for the rest of your life. They are better than any NASCAR moment on I-20. I guarantee!

CHAPTER 28

I Can't Believe I Missed!

For as long as I can remember, my dad took me to shoot skeet or clay pigeons, as he often referred to them. This would take place before duck season every year in order to teach me how to wing shoot properly. I have done the same for my son. I still remember the first dove he shot out of the air and the first duck he shot out of the air. I have a pretty good memory when it comes down to my hunts. My wife finds it interesting that I can remember what happened in a duck blind when I was eight but can't remember what she asked me to pick up at Walmart without a text message list. Oh, well, I digress. Skeet shooting is always a great way to tune up for the upcoming season. As much as that helps, it never ceases to amaze me how many of those *easy* shots I miss every year. I remember many of them just as much as I remember some of the great ones. (Even though the misses far outweigh the great shots).

For example: Great morning with my dad. It was not too cold but not too warm. The birds were flying, and one gorgeous green head mallard sat right down in the decoys off my side of the blind. I was only about eight or nine years old, and I had my single shot .410-gauge shotgun. I remember my dad telling me to take my time and shoot for the head. The duck was close—this was an easy shot even for me, and this trophy bird sat on the water not knowing what was about to hit him. As it turned out, nothing hit him, and he flew away.

Cold morning in Jones, Louisiana. The birds were moving pretty good when out on the horizon came a lone snow goose. Snow geese in the area don't exactly decoy very well, but this one was coming right in on my end of the blind. We all sat still and waited for the right time to call the shot. As I saw his landing gear come down, I called the shot. My shot was the first to ring out as I was the closest. All I remember is seeing my shot pattern scatter across the water beneath the bird and watch him turn as the others got their turn. They didn't miss like I did.

The birds were about to light on the other side of the water near the tree line when I gave them a loud series of notes on the call. The mallards picked up out of their landing pattern and made a turn toward our decoy spread. The trio made a pass behind us and then came around the end. Between my buddy Kyle and me, five shots rang out before the sixth finally got him at about sixty yards. The easy became the difficult very quickly.

A beautiful November morning was breaking. A family affair was taking place in the duck blind as I had my dad, my son, and my nephew with me. As I scanned for birds, I noticed a bird flying toward the blind at Mach one speed. I had but one shot, and I took it. I think I may have been twenty feet behind this bird as it sped past me. As things go in the wild, this bird took a wide turn and came by on the other end of the blind and ran into several wads of steel, much to his demise. Of all the birds I have killed, I never have gotten a redhead. As my dog brought this bird back, I realized I missed a pretty good chance at a beautiful drake. The bird now resides on my dad's wall at his house.

There really are more misses than I care to tell anyone about. I guess that is why we often use the phrase, "That's why we call it hunting and not killing." Even the best guys miss every now and then. Heck, I guess everyone misses.

Chapter 6 in the book of Romans in the New Testament records these words, *"For the wages of sin is death, but the gift of God is eternal life in Christ Jesus our Lord"* (Romans 6:23 NIV). The term *sin* in the Bible refers to *missing the mark*. A visual picture for the hunter is seeing what you have your sights set on but missing what you are aiming for. In life we strive to do good things and live a good life, but every single person at some time has missed the mark. We all have sin in our lives. I have no problem admitting that.

When you break this verse down into everyday language, it goes something like this: That which each of us earns because we failed to do what was right is death, but God, because He loves us, desires to give us a gift, something we didn't earn, and that gift is *eternal life*. This can only be possible because of what Jesus did on a cross two thousand years ago as He died in our place so that we could be forgiven and have a real lasting relationship with Him. Now that was a mouthful, but are the most important words I could ever share.

If you have never asked God to be a part of your life, now is as good a time as any. Just stop what you are doing and say a prayer that goes something like this:

Heavenly Father,
I want to have you in my life. I need you in my life. I am asking that today you will forgive those things that I have done wrong in my life and be a part of me from this day forward. I want to thank you for loving me and thank you for saving me. Help me to live with you and for you from now on. In Jesus name I pray. Amen.

These are the most important words you will ever say, and I hope that you have now said them to God. Find the contact info in this book and contact me with any questions that I can help answer for you or just to let me know of your decision to follow Jesus today.

As much as I have missed while hunting, this is one I didn't miss out on. I hope you don't miss this chance. It really is a game changer.

CHAPTER 29

Get Fired Up

It was one of those days where the wind would just bite your head off if you stuck it up out of the blind. We were in a pit blind in Louisiana with the temperatures somewhere in the low twenties. The temperature wasn't actually the problem. We had arrived at camp the evening before wearing short-sleeve shirts and blue jeans. Not long after we got unloaded and settled in, the front edge of a weather system arrived. There was a northern push coming through that brought torrential rains, heavy winds, and the threat of tornadoes. It rained and stormed all night long, almost until the time to get up and get ourselves ready. As most of you know, after the storm comes the cold. The temperatures dropped by about thirty-five degrees in a matter of hours. The north wind was twenty to thirty miles per hour and felt like it was cutting right through you. It was that kind of day.

On this particular trip, my hunting partner, Chuck, was fortunate enough to get to bring his father who was in his mid seventies at the time. We knew his dad by several names, including his given name of Frank, but also by Papa T, Buddy Boy, and Old Coot, just to name a few. Papa T, as many called him, was an avid hunter all of his life, and it was a joy to not only have him on the trip with us, but also to have the opportunity to sit in a blind with him and share in some great moments. On this particular day, however, it was extremely cold and Papa T was a very thin man. Unlike some of us in the blind, he had very little natural insulation, if you get my drift. As cold as it was, no one was talking about firing up one of the propane heaters we had in the blind. As I sat next to Papa T throughout the morning, I could see that he was cold, but when I asked him, he would always tell me he was fine. As the morning progressed I noticed that he had begun to shiver ever so slightly. In an attempt to not draw attention to him, I got Chuck's attention and told him that I was getting cold on my end of the blind and had him get the heater out and pass it down to me. I fired up that bad boy, placed it between Papa T and myself, and enjoyed warming up to it as much as he did.

It didn't take long to get warmed up and get back to watching for birds as there were many ducks and geese in the area that had pushed down with the front. As we sat in that old A-frame blind, looking to the sky for any birds that were willing to work into our decoy spread, I began to smell something that was out of the ordinary. It smelled a bit like burning rubber. As I looked around I noticed that Papa T had snuggled up a little too close to the heater and although he wasn't touching it, the heat coming off of it was indeed starting to melt a spot on his neoprene waders. Everything kind of happened quickly as others noticed the smell as well. I moved both the heater and Papa T as we all realized what was happening, and no one laughed any harder about it that he did. He went from being very cold to very, very hot in no time.

As I have reminisced about this story through the years, I have thought numerous times about how funny that situation was. It also has made me think about something else that is not funny but actually a little sad. There is a verse in the book of Revelation, the last book in the Bible, that says; "I know your deeds, that you are neither cold nor hot. I wish you were either one or the other" (Revelation 3:15 NIV).

God is very clear. He doesn't want people who are lukewarm in their relationship with Him. He wants people who are hot. He wants people who are on fire for Him. I believe this is vitally important to every man. Men need to understand that following God with a lukewarm attitude can be damaging to themselves and to their family as well as to the people inside their circle of influence. What this world needs, what this country needs, and what the families in this country need are men who are willing to stand up for what they say they believe in. Our sons need that kind of role model so that in turn they go into our society as positive contributors to all that they get involved in. We need our daughters to see in us the kind of man they need to get involved with and eventually settle down with as they start their own families. Our churches need men who are not ashamed to say with their words and echo those words with their lives that the God who created ducks and duck hunting and everything else we see and know is the God that controls our lives. When we get that fired up for God, I promise you, amazing things will happen at every level.

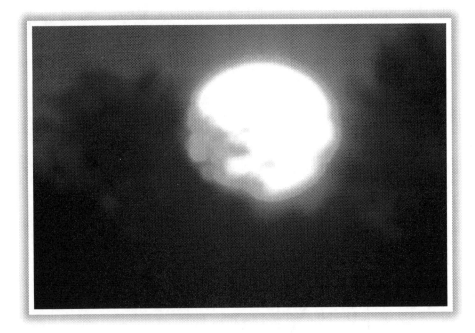

My good friend and duck guide Johnny Wink has a saying that he uses constantly, and that phrase is "Get fired up!" I will use that same phrase as it applies to your relationship with God: get fired up! He wants you hot, not lukewarm. Examine what you need to do to make that happen. Envision the positive impact that will have on your life and the lives of the people around you. Ask God to show you what He wants and how you can get there. Then hang on for the ride because the journey is going to be incredible.

*** The picture in this chapter looks a little strange, I know, but it is one that I took of the sun rising over a flooded field one morning. I zoomed in as far as I could and this is what I got. To me, it shows the intensity of the sun and reminds me that our lives ought to reflect that same intensity for God. *Get fired up.*

CHAPTER 30

Just Do It!

As I mentioned in a previous story, there was an old trapper named Jim that lived in an old cabin way back in the woods on the edge of the swamp and marsh. I don't really know how my grandfather met him or how long my dad had known him. I do know that every time that I went hunting back in that area, we had to stop and see Jim on the way out. We would give him part of the day's kill since Jim lived primarily off the land. When I would go see my grandfather on weekends or during the summer when I would stay with him, we would get in the car and go from Paradis up the road a few miles to Boutte, turn off the main road, and travel back down the shell-covered roads to where Jim's little cabin was. My grandfather would always stop at the store and get a bag of those little orange sliced candies to give to Jim. When we would get to the cabin, we would honk to let him know we were there. If it was summer, we would sit on the porch and visit. If it was winter, we would go inside by the pot belly stove and keep warm. Jim always had interesting stories to tell and he would always listen to me tell mine. Many adults don't want to hear a small kid talk, but Jim always wanted to hear me. I remember so many things about the cabin: how he cooked, what he ate, the rustic bed, the stove, and the old shotguns that were in the corner. He would let me shoot the old .410-gauge shotgun outside. That gun had seen too much in its time. Even still, it was one of Jim's favorite guns. I remember things about Jim as well. He was an older black man with white hair and white whiskers. He was a trapper, and most importantly he was a World War I veteran. I don't remember the exact stories of the war, but I remember being in awe of those stories. Jim had very few friends. The reason was probably that very few people knew he was back there. My grandfather was his friend and went to check on him all the time. If my memory serves me right, I believe when Jim passed away, it was my grandfather who found him and made sure that he was taken care of with dignity and respect. That is exactly what he deserved.

As I reflect on going to see Jim all those times, I remember the words spoken by Jesus found in the book of Matthew, which is the first book in the New Testament. In Matthew chapter 7, Jesus says, "So in everything, do to others what you would have them do to you" (Matthew 7:12 NIV).

This verse has come to be known as the Golden Rule. Do unto others as you would have them do unto you. That is a pretty good rule to live by. What if we as men started to apply that verse, that principle to our spouses? What kind of transformation do you think might take place? What about at work? Do you think the environment that we work in would change if this principle was applied? What about in our parenting or in our relationships with our neighbors? Let's take that a little farther. What would happen if we applied that teaching to the people who wait on our tables, bag our groceries, change our oil, assist us in stores, or take care of any menial task that needs to be done? Jesus wants us to apply this principle across the board to all people with whom we have any contact. I have learned after doing what I do for twenty-five years that every person has something they are dealing with. You never know what difference you will make when you begin to treat all people the very same way you want to be treated. Notice it doesn't say to treat people the way you are treated. It does, however, say to treat them the way *you want to be treated*. I promise that when you begin this application, you will see tremendous results in the way you feel and the way that you are treated in return. Go out there are make a difference by doing random acts of kindness. Your life will never be the same!

CONTACT INFORMATION

Jonathan S. Porter

RevJono@aol.com

On Facebook @ Jonathan Porter, Greenville, GA

Or on Facebook @ Beyond the Blind

Twitter @Beyondtheblind